BUDDHISM

THE SPIRITUAL LINEAGE OF DZOGCHEN MASTERS

BUDDHISM
THE SPIRITUAL LINEAGE OF DZOGCHEN MASTERS

KARMA WANGCHUK

ANMOL PUBLICATIONS PVT. LTD.
NEW DELHI-110 002 (INDIA)

Distributor

M/S PE KHANG ENTERPRISES
Luger Theatre Complex, P. O. Box No. 460
Thimphu, Bhutan

Buddhism: The Spiritual Lineage of Dzogchen Masters

First Edition, 1998
Reprint, 2003
ISBN 81-7488-669-9

PRINTED IN INDIA

Published by J. L. Kumar for Anmol Publications Pvt. Ltd., New Delhi-110 002 in arrangement with Dr. Karma Wangchuk, Asstt. Director/Research Officer, National Library, P. O. Box 185, Thimphu, Bhutan and Printed at Mehra Offset Press, Delhi.

Contents

སྲོལ་འཛིན་ལྷན་ཚོགས།

SPECIAL COMMISSION
FOR CULTURAL AFFAIRS

FOREWORD

The study of biographies of the Dzogchen Masters is a fascinating branch of the discipline of Buddhist studies. A great deal of literature belonging to the Nyingma tradition deals with their lives and teachings, which no students of Buddhism can afford to ignore. The record of their lives and teachings constitute an important source of our knowledge of Buddhist history, religion and philosophy.

The Dzogchen Masters profess the secret Doctrine called *Dzogchen Nyingthig* which embodies the essence of Buddha's teachings. This secret doctrine is perpetuated and transmitted from one lineage member to the next, from Guru to disciple, in an unbroken succession, maintaining the continuity of blessing and experiences.

One such scholar and master was Longchen Rabjampa, who is well known to the Bhutanese people since he established eight monasteries, called *Ling,* in Bhutan. Most of the monasteries are in use even today as meditation centers and places of higher studies, or *Shedra,* like Tharpaling. Kunkhen Longchen Rabjampa, one of the greatest of all Nyingma masters compiled and systematized the Khandro Nyingthig and Vima Nyingthig teachings in his Longchen Nyingthig and transmitted his teachings to the

སྲོལ་འཛིན་ལྷན་ཚོགས།

SPECIAL COMMISSI
FOR CULTURAL AFFAI

people. He was the founder and initiator of the Nyingthig tradition in Bhutan. Many Bhutanese disciples practice the *Khandro Nyingthig*. According to the scriptures, he was reincarnated as the great Terton Pemalingpa in order to reveal the remaining parts of his treasures for the benefit of all sentient beings.

Dr. Karma Wangchuk's preliminary study of the lives and teachings of the Dzogchen Masters is a pioneering work by a Bhutanese scholar. It is based on traditionally handed-down manuscripts dating from the 8th century. The present work, though small in volume, will certainly facilitate a better understanding of the nature of Buddhism in contemporary Bhutan. I am sure his work will open a new area of study and research in the history of Buddhism in our country.

31th October,1997
Thimphu, Bhutan

Dago Tshering
CHAIRMAN
Special Commission for
Cultural Affairs

སྲོལ་འཛིན་ལྷན་ཚོགས།

SPECIAL COMMISSION
FOR CULTURAL AFFAIRS

PREFACE

All beings wish to be happy and free from misery. Although scientific development, modern weapons and abundant material progress may alleviate the temporary effects of dissatisfaction, such external means can never totally eradicate its fundamental cause. the true solution is to cultivate deep human compassion, love and respect for others. Whether a person is a Buddhist or a Hindu, a follower of a specific religion or simply a believer in non-violence and morality, good human qualities such as kindness, generosity, humility and compassion are preferred by all. By cultivating such altruistic and beneficial attributes, the cause of suffering, self-cherishing, will gradually diminish. This, in turn, will promote unity and harmony among human beings of all nations.

In Buddhist teachings, compassion, the wish that all beings may be separated from their suffering, plays an especially important part. In order to help others to become free from misery, Buddha taught that the most effective way is to attain the fully purified state beyond sorrow (Nirvana). The wish to do so for the sake of oneself and all others is known as the "enlightened motivation of the awakening mind" (Bodhicitta*)*. The source of this highest teaching is found in the Nyingma, or Old, School, and is known as the Great Completion, or Dzogpa Chenpo (Mahasandi), or as the Atiyoga direct method for realizing the nature of the mind and attaining Buddhahood. The *Nyingthig, or the "Essence of the Heart,"* teachings precisely explain the various methods for directly actualizing the innermost teachings of the Dzogpa Chenpo. The Dzogchen Nyingthig, as a teaching, fundamentally deals with the expression of the doctrine of three Kayas, or the three perfection Bodies of a fully Awakened Being, and they have arisen through the Three Systems of spiritual transmission.

The first is known as the *Mind Transmission* of the Buddha. The second level of spiritual transmission is known as the *Knowledge-Holders Indication System.* The third system of spiritual transmission of the Dzogchen lineage is that known as the *Audial Transmission* of the yogis. This form of spiritual transmission in Tibet and Bhutan initially spread through two lineages in the beginning and early part of the ninth century. One originated from Vimalamitra and the other from Guru Rinpoche. Vimalamitra transmitted the teachings to Nyang Tingzin Zangpo and other disciples. From Nyang this unbroken lineage of audial transmission came down to Longchen Rabjam; the other lineage, from Guru Rinpoche, was passed on to his disciples, the dakini Yeshe Tshogyal and Princess Pemasal. The texts for these teachings were mystically concealed by Guru Rinpoche, to be unearthed later for the benefit of his disciples. These were later discovered by a male incarnation of the Princess, the Trulku Pema Ley Drail Tshal, by his next incarnation as Longchen Rabjampa, and by his further incarnation as Pema Lingpa, and so on.

Dr. Karma Wangchuk has carefully compiled the Biographies of the Dzogchen Nyingthig Masters of these incarnations, first into Dharma language (chos skad) and then into English. To introduce it to scholars who work in English,

སྲོལ་འཛིན་ལྷན་ཚོགས།

SPECIAL COMMISSION FOR CULTURAL AFFAIRS

his translation is both lucid and faithful to the original. The work is balanced by an historical Introduction at the beginning and critical notes at the end.

I hope this volume will contribute to the literature of Buddhist doctrine.

10th October,1997
Thimphu, Bhutan

Sangay Wangchuk
SECRETARY
Special Commission for
Cultural Affairs

Acknowledgments

This book, The Spiritual Lineage of Dzogchen Masters, is based on my Ph.D. thesis, submitted to Delhi University in 1994.

Throughout the compilation, translation and writing this book, I have been extremely fortunate to benefit from correspondence and fruitful discussions with friends and colleagues, philosophers and practitioners. I would like to thank the venerable Professor Thegcho, who lent his vast learning to me and provided me with his own copies of the texts; the Venerable Trulku Thamched Khenpa; Gonpo Trulku; Lama Namdrel Zangpo who first urged me to publish this book in English; the very Venerable Nyolchu Khen Rinpoche, who has given me much helpful encouragement and spiritual support; Mrs. Suzanne Lhemery and Mrs. Sylvie Junca, whose goodwill toward my work I hold in high regard; and my friends Gelong Thinley Dhendup, Lam Dampa Minjur, Dr. Yonten Dargye, Mr. Ugyen Tenzin, Mr. Tshering Tenzin, and others too many to name, who assisted me in so many ways.

I would like to acknowledge Geshe Gelek Gyatsho; my Ph.D. supervisor, Prof. K.K.Mittal; Prof. Sanghasena Singh; Prof. K.T.S.Sarao; Associate Prof. Dawa Norbu, all of whom shared their vast learning with me in numerous ways.

I would like to extend my humble gratitude and respect to the Home Minister, H.E. Lyonpo Dago Tshering, for his benevolent guidance and support and for writing the Forward to this volume.

I express my sincere gratitude to Dasho Tshewang Rigxin, Dasho Khandu Wangchuk, Dasho Pema Wangchen, Dasho Sangay Ngedup, Dasho Karma Letho, Dasho Jigme Thinley, Dasho Thinley Gyamtsho, Dasho (Dr.) Kingzang Dorji and Dasho Tashi Phuntshog, for their appreciation, helpful encouragement and support.

I owe my special thanks and gratitude to Mr. Sangay Wangchuk for his Preface and for his unfailing encouragement and loving kindness. I am grateful to my friend Prof. Mark Mancall of standfort University, who gave so generously of his time in editing and also clarifying various points. The author is solely responsible for any mistakes or omissions in this work.

I would like to thank, and apologize to, all the illustrators, authors and publishers for using some of their artwork and illustrations without permission.

I also remember, and take this opportunity to extend my salutations and best regards to, all my teachers who have continuously inspired and guided me throughout my academic life.

Finally, I thank Peter Koenig, Resident Coordinator of Helvetas in Bhutan, Manfred Deimel and Druk Sherig Tenzin, for their generous financial contributions toward the publication of this book. Last but by no means least, I thank my parents, Daisy & Nyima Lhamo Wangchuk, whose love and encouragement have been the sustaining force in the publication of this book.

Karma Wangchuk

INTRODUCTION

ཆོས་ལོངས་སྤྲུལ་གསུམ།

The Vajrayana Buddhist tradition known as 'Absolute Perfection of *Heart Drop 'Dzogchen Nyingthig '(rdzogs chen snying thig)* has been practiced in many areas,[1] but it reached its pinnacle of development in Tibet and Bhutan. From the time of Padmasambhava (Guru Rinpoche) to the present,[2] this tradition has been maintained and enhanced by various Gurus from both Tibet and Bhutan.

Before the spread of Buddhism in the Himalayan region, the Tibetan people practiced the Bön religion,[3] at least from the period of the first King, Nyathri Tsanpo (gnya' thri btsan po, 147 B.C.E.) to Oggi Tsan ('og gis btsan, 5th century).[4] However, during the reign of King Lha Thothori Nyen Zhal (b. 433), who was a descendent of Nyathri Tsanpo, a casket containing three different texts fell from heaven. This casket was named 'Sacred Helper. Nyanpo Sangwa (bsnyan po bsang ba) and the event marked the first introduction of Buddhism into Tibet. It was only during the reign of the most popular King, Songtsan Gampo (srong btsan sgam po, 617?-50), the fifth successor to Lha Thothori Nyen Zhal, that the spread of Buddhism gained momemtum in the region. Buddhism's Golden Age in Tibet dates from the reign of King Thrisong Detsan (756-797 CE). He was one of the three famous "Religious Kings" of Tibet and is considered to be the reincarnation of Manjushri.[5] From his youth, the King exhibited a strong inclination toward Buddhism. He invited Bodhisattva Shantarakshita (mkhen kun byang chub sems pa zhi ba 'tsho, 700 CE - ?)[6] and Padmasambhava to come from India and, with the help of these masters, he introduced the first monastic order into Tibet.[7] He was also responsible for the founding of the first monastery, Samye (sam yas mi gyur lhun drub), in 763 CE. This monastery was built in the shape of a mandala, on the model of Odantapuri Mahavihara at Bihar in India. It is said that when Padmasambhava blessed the images and pictures inside the temple, they came alive. "Samyas can be regarded as the symbol of the Sun from which the rays of Dharma spread all over Tibet in the Course of time...Hitherto Buddhism in Tibet was like lightening in a dark sky. It appeared for some time and disappeared. It was only after the successful completion of Samye monastery that Buddhism got deeply implanted in Tibet. The credit for firmly planting the banner of Buddhism in Tibet goes to Guru Padmasambhava, popularly known as Guru Rinpoche. The Dharma introduced by the Guru was not branded as any sect. It was a pure Dharma."[8] King Thrisong Detsan also invited Vimalamitra,[9] one of the foremost of five hundred great Panditas,[10] along with many other great Indian scholars and sages, to Tibet. He brought together many very learned Tibetan translators (lo tsa wa) who were considered incarnations of Buddhas and Bodhisattvas.[11] Among them were Vairocana,[12] Kawa Paltsek (ska ba dpal brtsegs), Cogro Klu'i Gyaltshan,[13] and many others (all these flourished in the Eighth Century). These great Panditas and scholars translated numerous Buddhist canonical works into Tibetan.

Before the introduction of Buddhism, the Bhutanese also practiced the Bön religion. In Bhutan, however, the new faith did not come into any serious conflict with Bön as it did in Tibet. Therefore, the advent of Buddhism in Bhutan was a peaceful and evolutionary process, and it ushered in the dawn of a new spiritual and historical consciousness in the country.

Buddhism was first introduced into Bhutan in the Seventh Century CE, when the Tibetan King Songtsan Gampo undertook the construction of Kichu temple at Paro and Jampa Temple in Bumthang as missionary projects.

In Bhutan, as in Tibet, Buddhism continued to evolve even after its introduction. The culmination of this historical process took place in the early Eighth Century, when King Sindu Raja (lcags khar) of Bumthang invited Guru Padmasambhava to subdue Shilging Karpo, the spirit that had caused the king to become seriously ill. The Guru met the king and subdued the power of Shilging Karpo and of other evil spirits as well; the king was cured. Thereafter, Padmasambhava propagated Buddhism in Bhutan, and in the course of time it became the dominant religion in the country. "Guru Padmasambhava is a great historical and religious figure in Bhutan, embodying almost all of its religious, ethical and national legends. He is worshipped in his eight-fold manifestation." Bhutanese believe that Padmasambhava is still accessible today, assuming various manifestations to help those of this age.

The national religion of Bhutan is Drukpa Kagyu (brug pa bka' brgyud),[14] but the majority of Bhutanese still practice *Dzogpa Chenpo*. They believe that it is the only religion that can easily transform immediate bodily existence into the form of light, without undergoing hardship for many years and eons.

Each word of the name *Dzogpa Chenpo Longchen Nyingthig* has significance and helps explain the basic characteristics of this teaching. *(rDzogs), 'perfection,'* means that there is no higher practice. It refers to the perfection of the 'five paths' and 'ten grounds' of Mahayana Buddhism and suggests all the auspicious qualities of the Buddhas and Bodhisattvas.[15]

Chen, 'great,' signifies that there is no greater or more expansive teaching than this one and that this teaching belongs to the Mahayana (Greater Vehicle) and, for certain practitioners, to the Hinayana (Lesser Vehicle) form of Buddhism. The Mahayana has two paths: sutra and Tantra.[16] The great Perfection (rdzogs chen) teaches both, and it contains the full meaning of all sutras and Tantras, but it itself is included within the tantric path. The words *Klong Chen, 'Vast Openness,'* suggest the openness (klong) of the thought of the Truth Body (Dharmakaya) as well as of all conqueror Buddhas. Because this openness is limitless, it is called great or vast.

The thought of the Buddha has three forms: the *Truth Body (Dharmakaya),* the *Complete Enjoyment Body (Sambhogakaya),* and the *Emanation Body (Nirmanakaya).* The Truth Body is the body of emptiness that is beyond all elaboration's of thought; it is the ultimate truth fully realized. The Truth Body, which is the nature of Peace, has passed beyond all conceptions of subject and object; it is a state in which all elaborations of thought have been extinguished; the Complete Enjoyment Body arises from its essence. The Truth Body is like a clear glass, and the light coming from it is the Complete Enjoyment Body, a pure and eternal manifestation in the form of the highest truth. Emanations from the Complete Enjoyment Body manifest themselves in any form necessary to tame and to help sentient beings. Each such manifestation is an instance of an Emanation Body.

There are special female deities known as 'mothers'

ཅོག་རོ་ཀླུའི་རྒྱལ་མཚན།

or 'Sky-Goers,' for whom this teaching is as precious as the essence of their own hearts. To those who cherish it, it is known as the *'Heart Drop' (snying thig).*

The Dzogchen teachings came from the area of the Dhana Kosa Lake in the western country of Uddiyana.[17] The basic text of the Dzogchen (Atiyoga) system is called the *Nyingthig Yazhi (snying thig ya bzhi),* and the basic philosophical background of this system rests on the doctrine of the *Madhyamika* as developed by the Indian Panditas, Nagarjuna and Aryadeva.[18] The master Jampal Shenyen received the Dzogchen transmission from the first representative of the Human-tradition, Garab Dorje (dga' rab do rje), in a golden box.[19] He then summarized the 6,400,000 Tantras into three classes. a) Mind section *(sems sde),* b) the Unending Experience of Being *(klong sde),* and c) Guidance (man ngag sde). The most important of all the important teachings of *Man Ngak sde* section is the Nyingthig, which in turn is classified into *(bshad rgyud)* and *Narjud (rnar rgyud).*[20]

Guru Padmasambhava, Vimalamitra, Vairocana, Santaraksita and many other great saints and scholars gave teachings to those of superior faculties and taught them how to perform the Sadhanas.[21] The great Pandita Vimalamitra preached the general Buddhist teachings of the Sutras and the Tantras. By widely exposing fortunate followers to the particular teachings of the secret Dzogchen Nyingthig, Vimalamitra helped them attain rainbow bodies.[22] This doctrine has been continued from Guru to Guru through an unbroken chain of oral teachings known as the Nyingthig Kama (bka'ma).[23]

According to the Nyingthig Terma (gter ma) tradition,[24] the doctrine was transmitted by Sri-Simha to Guru Padmasambhava,[25] who had to consider four points: (1) the doctrine should not disappear; (2) its teachings should not be misunderstood; (3) its blessings should not disappear; and (4) its tradition should be maintained by a close lineage. With these considerations in mind, he formulated secret teachings showing the method of attaining perfection through the Tantras,[26] the method of achieving perfection through the core techniques,[27] and instructions on how to put the core techniques into practice,[28] along with the blessings,[29] the authority of initiation,[30] credentials of authority,[31] future prophecy,[32] and so on. In order to benefit sentient beings in the future, Guru Padmasambhava, together with Vairocana and Yeshe Tshogyal (Padmasambhava's consort and foremost disciple), concealed holy images and Dharmas, amrta and many blessed articles in ordinary places in the earth,[33] lakes, oceans, rocks and sky, as well as in extraordinary places, such as the four directions in Bhutan, Tibet, Nepal and China. These places were assigned to fortunate individuals who would excavate them at some future time. When the appropriate time arrived to help sentient beings, a series of blessed and fortunate individuals unearthed these treasures and propagated the doctrine. The *Dzogchen Nyingthig teachings ('Quintessential Instructions")* are classified into two aspects: *'Vima Nyingthig'* and *Khandro Nyingthig (mkha' gro snying thig),* also known as the *'the two mother Nyingthigs.* The former is Vimalamitra's concealed Nyingthig, which was unearthed by Neten Dangma Lhungyal. The latter refers to Padmasambhava's concealed treasure text, which was discovered by Pedma Ledreltsal (pad ma las 'brel' tsal). Their elaborate explanations and the explication of their

དཀའ་རབ་རྡོ་རྗེ།

secret meaning in condensed forms are called *Lama Yangthig (bla ma yang thig)* and *the Khandro Yangthig (mkha' 'gro yang thig*) respectively, and their combined secret essence is called the *Zabmo Yangthig.*

Padmasambhava demonstrated these teachings at the court of King Thrisong Detsan by bringing back to life Lhachi Pedmasal (lha lcam pedma gsal), the daughter of the King by one of his wives, Drok Za Jangchuk Don (brog bza byang chub sgron). He went to the dead child and wrote the syllabus Nri (ནྲྀ) on the girl's chest with red chalk dust. With intense meditative concentration, Guru Rinpoche brought the girl back to life. He then gave her an empowerment (dbang bskur) for the guidance of the spiritual holder of the Nyingthig teaching (man ngag mkha' 'gro'i snying thig). The Guru then concealed the precious Nyingthig teachings in a secret place, establishing their existence as Terma or 'buried treasure'. The secret teachings received by Kunkhen Drime 'Odzer (kun mkhyen dri me 'od zer) or Longche Rabjampa (klong chen rab byam pa (1308-1363), one of the greatest of all Nyingma masters, in the form of treasure concealed in the mind, are known as *The Earlier Nyingthig* tradition. The uninterrupted oral transmission of these teachings has continued to the present time in both Tibet and Bhutan. Pedma Lingpa (padma gling pa) (1450-1521C.E.), the Bhutanese 'King of Treasure-Revealers', who was the reincarnation of Kunkhen Drime 'Odzer, continued this tradition.

In the eighteenth century, the spiritual master Rigzin Jigme Lingpa (1729-1798),[34] an incarnation of the King Thrisong Detsan, received the complete Dzogchen Nyingthig teachings in a mystical vision from Guru Padmasambhava, Vimalamitra, Manjushrimitra and Longchen Rabjampa, through mind indication and audial transmission, in the state of pure vision. In his vision, he saw Longchen Rabjampa three times, received the blessings of being inseparable from the spiritual Master and thereby realized thc true state of perfect Accomplishment, or Buddhahood. He discovered the "Concealed Treasures of Dharma" (gter chos) of the Longchen Nyingthig and thus founded the tradition that takes this name. The Dzogchen Nyingthig and Longchen Nyingthig are known respectively as the earlier and later Nyingthig teachings.

First Dodrubchen Jigme Thinley 'Odzer ('jigs med thrin las 'od zer) 1745-1821) was consecrated Choe Dak (chos bdag) [principle holder] of the Longchen Nyingthig by Jigme Lingpa himself. But it was Jigme Kundrol ('jigs med kun drol, Dodrubchen's spiritual friend, who, after his education in Tibet, came back to Bhutan and propagated the teachings in his own homeland.

This Book is a study of how the Nyingthig Gong 'Og tradition has survived through oral transmission of the teaching from one lineage holder to another.

The author's purpose in writing this book is to convey both the real nature and feeling of Samsara and the urgent need to seek liberation for oneself and for others. This is why Tantric teaching is intended not only for those in monasteries but also for sincere lay devotees who properly maintain the secret vows and understand the special injunctions that are part of trantric teaching and practice. At the same time, one must remember that the secret Tantric teachings strictly warn against giving them to those who do not possess the foundation and the real understanding that are required. These warnings are stated for the benefit of both the giver and the receiver, so that neither will suffer untoward consequences and so that the Dharma may perpetually maintain its efficacy.

NOTES

1 The third major vehicle is the Vajrayana (rdor rje theg pa), the Vehicle of Tantra, which is specifically concerned with the practice of yoga. It is said that Sakyamuni manifested as Vjaradhara in order to teach Vajrayana.

2 Padmasambhava, popurlarly known as guru Rinpoche i.e., 'Precious one', the most reverential title of address for a lama, or

a very polite word to address a Lama, visited Tibet & Bhutan in the early 8th century C.E

3 See G.Tucci, The Religions of Tibet, Chapter vi

4 See skya Bla ma Dam pa bsod nams rgyal mtshan, rgyal rabs gsal ba'i me long, p.129

5 *Jam dpal dbyang*, Manjushri; the embodiment of the loving-Kindness of all the Buddha. at the time of Buddha Sakyamuni he manifested as a Bodhisattva disciple. In the future he will manifest as the fifth universal Buddha.

6 *Zhiwa tsho or mkhen kun byang chub sems pa*, Santaraksita; was born about 700 AD to the royal family in Zahor (Bengal) in the small village of Sabhar during the reign of Gopala, the first king of the Pala Dynasty.

7 Va Vrizig, Ba Salnang, Pagor Vairocana, Nganlam Gyalwa Chogyang, Marin Chenchog, Khen Lui Wangpo sungwa and Lasum Gyalwa Changchub.

8 Bhutia, Dr.T.D.; Beyond Eternity Through Mysticism, Dolma Dorji Lhaden, Darjeeling, 1994, p.135.

9 Vimalamitra was born in Western India 3rd century CE and began his studies in the Vajrayana under the Acarya Buddhaguhya (Sangs rgyas gsang ba). He then journeyed to China, where he studied for nine years with Sri Simha, receiving the inner, outer, and secret cycles of the oral-transmission (snyan brgyud) of the Atiyoga.

10 Pandits are of two kinds, ordinary pandits and great pandits. One who possesses the knowledge of the five minor sciences is an ordinary pandit. One who possesses the knowledge of all the ten sciences (five minor and five major) is a great or Maha pandit. The five major sciences are: language, logic, arts, medicine and scriptures (of Buddha).

11 *byang chub sems pa*, Bodhisattvas; are those great beings whose only aim is to attain Enlightenment for the benefit of all sentient beings.

12 *rnam par snags mdzad*, Vairocana; was born of the spa or Clan in the fertile valley of snye mo bye mkhas, which lies between rgyal rtse (Gyantse) and Lhasa. One of Padmasambhava's three most important disciples, he was also one of the original seven monks (sad mi) ordained by Santaraksita. He received the principal lineage of the Mahayoga from Buddhaguhya and the esoteric transmission from his teacher Sri Simha.

13 Cog ro klu'i rgyal mtshen and ska ba dpal brtsegs, 8th century C.E, went to India on the order of King Thri Song Detsen to invite Vimalamitra to teach the quintessence of the Buddhadharma to the Royal Court

14 Drukpa Kagyud is the name of the school to which Marpa, Milarepa and Gampopa belonged.

15 The practitioner's way to enlightenment traditionally arranged into five paths *(lam lnga):* Tshogs lam ; path of accumulation, sbyor lam; path of unification, mthong lam; path of seeing, sgom lam ; path of meditation, and mthar phyin pa'i lam, mi slob pa'i lam; path of fulfillment or of no more learning.

Bhumi; (tib. Sa; earth, stage, level, ground) The Bhumi are the stage of relaxation on the Bodhisattva path, usually enumerated ten: (1) Pramudita (Very Joyous stage), (2) Vimala (stainless),(3) Prabhakari (luminous), (4) Arcismati (radiant stage),(5) sudurjaya (difficult to overcome), (6) Abhimukhi (turned towards Bodhi or Approaching), (7) Duramgami (Far going stage), (8) Acala (Immovable stage), (9) Sadhumati (stage of good thoughts0, (10) Dharma-megha (cloud of the Law)

16 *mdo,* Sutra; the sutras are those Hinayana and Mahayana texts in the Buddhist canon that are attributed to Sakyamuni Buddha. They are found in the bka' gyur. Sutra means meeting point, junction, referring to the meeting of Buddha's enlightenment and the student's understanding.

rgyud, Tantra; may refer to many different kinds of texts. For instance, there are medical tantras, astrological tantras, and so on. More specifically, tantra refers to the root texts of the Vajrayana and to the systems of meditation they describe. Tantras, similar to Sutras, are attributed to Sakyamuni Buddha, who sometimes manifests as Vajradhara, Vajrasattva and so on. Tantra means continuity and refers to continuity throughout the ground, path and fruition of the journey.

17 *O-rgyen,* Uddiyana; is the ancient kingdom of the Swat valley in Northern Pakistan, Before the Muslim invasion it was a centre of Tantric Practice, and as Guru Pema's birth place it became known as the Dakini Paradise, *Nirmanakaya* Buddhafield (O-rgyen mkha' 'gro gling).

18 *Klu-sGrub*, Nagarjuna; was born in Vidarba to a Brahmin family of Southern India, sometime in the First and Second Century AD He was the founder of the Madhyamika school. His name came

from the legend that he retrieved the Prajnaparamita literature from the nagas.

Phags pa lha, Aryadeva; the foremost disciple of the Acarya Nagarjuna, was miraculously born from a lotus flower in a garden of the king of Singala (according to legend). This may be Sri Lanka.

19 *Jam pal Shey nyen, Manjushrimitra*; studied with dgra' rab rdo rje for seventy-five years and received innumerable instructions in the Dharma, including the whole of the Dzogchen Atiyoga system, which was directly transmitted to him from the mind of rdo rje sems dpa by way of the voice of his teacher.

dga' rab rdo rje (b. 55 AD) was born in the country of Uddiyana, near Dhanakosha Lake. rdo rje sems dpa' transmitted the bka' ma, which originated in the Dharmakaya, to him.

20 *bshad rgyud* 'explanatory Tantra'

rnar rgyud 'mouth to ear Tantra'

21 *sgrub thabs*, *Sadhanas;* (1) a liturgical meditation text; (2) a cycle or regular and frequent practice of any *yoga* or meditation; (3) method for attainment associated with a tantric deity.

22 *Ja lus*, Rainbow body; the rainbow body is achieved by realizing the impure material body as a body of light.

23 *bka' ma* tradition is the continuous transmission of teachings, texts, practices, sadhanas, and realizations that have passed from teacher to student in an unbroken succession since the time of Buddha's word. It is the Adi-Buddha, Kun tu bzang po (Samantabhadra), who teaches the bka-Ma, which are essentially timeless and yet appear in all times and in all the ten directions.

24 *gter ma* are the precious sacred articles and Dharmas which were hidden until the time was appropriate for their revealing. These Terma were hidden by Padmasambhava and other Tertons.

25 Sri Simha was born in the year 289 AD in the country known as 'the black expanse' (western China, or Khotan) to a wise and virtuous householder. He was the disciple of Manjushrimitra.

26 *sgrub thabs*

27 *Man ngag*

28 *Lag len*

29 *sman lam*

30 *dbang bskur*

31 *gtad rgya*

32 *Lung bsten*

33 *Amrita (bdud rtsi*; the drink of deathlessness) blessed liquor, used in Vajrayana meditation practices, to purify defilements.

34 Here, a knowledge-holder *(Rig-'Dzin; Vidyadhara*), a being who has direct and pure vision of the nature of reality, manifests to a receptive disciple and transmits the teaching by mean of pronouncing a mantra or showing a sign. In this system the complete verbal empowerment and instructions are transmitted by word of mouth from practitioner to practitioner.

35 *Gong-'Og* (earlier and later sNying-thig teachings) i.e., The rdzogs chen snying thig and Klong chen sNying-thig.

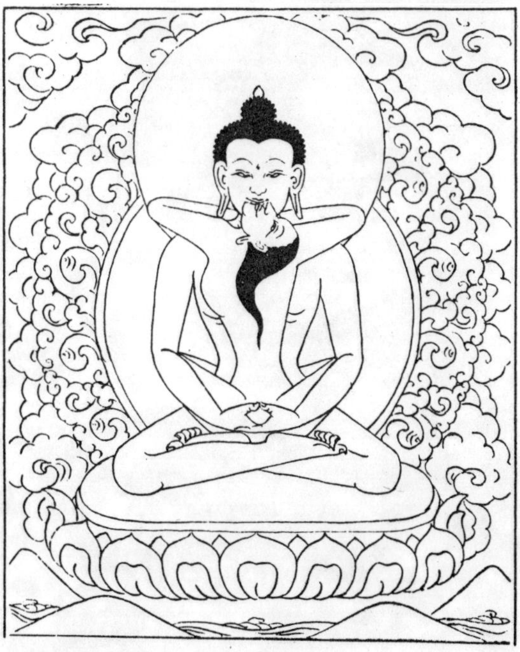

Kun-tu-bzang-po

14

CHAPTER ONE

LHACI PEMASAL : THE FIRST EMBODIMENT OF KUNKHEN LONGCHEN RABJAMPA

Padmasambhava, also known as Guru Rinpoche, brought Buddhism to Tibet and Bhutan. The seeds of Buddhism in general, and of *Dzogchen Nyingthig (rdzogs chen snying thig*) in particular, were further nourished by various incarnations in Tibet and Bhutan. This chapter concerns not only the present life but also the previous and future births of Lhaci Pemasal (lha gcig padma gsal), the first embodiment of Kunkhen (kun mkhyen). The sources are mostly in the form of questions and answers between Padmasambhava and King Thrisong Detsan (thri srong lde btsan), in which Padmasambhava explains to the King the cause of the untimely death of Lhaci Pemasal and makes many others predictions.

Prayer of supplication

This is a brief account of where the Guru and Yeshe Tshogyal (ye she mtsho rgyal) dwelt and what they did during those days.

While Padmasambhava and his consort Yeshe Tshogyal at Zho Teyte Drodrag (zho stod te sgro brag) were on a retreat, the wisdom dakinis admonished her that the mind of the incarnated body of the great Guru possessed the profound instruction called *Heart drop (Nyingthig)* and following this instruction strictly for three years would bring liberation within this life. Therefore, they instructed her to request the Guru to reveal the secret teaching for the welfare of sentient beings. She immediately arranged great offerings and said, "O great Guru, please reveal to us the profound instruction of the *Heart drops*, which can liberate us within this very life." She prostrated herself and made many circumambulation. The Guru Rinpoche replied, "What you said was excellent." This instruction differs from earlier Buddhist teachings in Tibet and goes beyond all the nine *Yanas.*[1]

> *By perceiving the root meaning of 'Nyingthig',*
> *the teaching of Dzogchen,*
> *the projection of our view and meditation vanished.*
> *Without any hardship we can complete the paths and Bhumis (sa, lam).*
> *Without spiritual knowledge and artificial modification, one can free oneself from ignorance.*
> *Without generation by cause, one can obtain the result.*
> *For a moment appear, 'dgongs pa' the mind treasure miraculously.*

"We can transform this body of aggregates into the illuminated *'Sambhogakaya' (longs sku)* in this life itself. After having wandered for three years in the abode of 'Og min,[2] you will come to know that there is also an instruction to keep the Kingdom in the Heaven of the *Dharmakaya (chos sku)";* having said this, he promised to explicate these teachings in a big Congregation Hall. Having opened the mandala of '*Zhi khro don' the peaceful and wrathful deities*, Guru gave the complete initiation of empowerment and verbal authorization to a hundred thousand wisdom Dakinis, including a Consort called Khar Chen Za' (yeshe tshogyal).

ཡེ་ཤེས་མཚོ་རྒྱལ།

Thereafter, he also gave them many instructions about the seventeenth and eighteenth volumes of Tantras, and the Tantras of *Longsel Nima (klong gsal nyima),* which are in the eighteenth volume. Finally, the Guru and Yeshe Tshogyal selected the most comprehensive instruction of the Tantras. They also selected the *Kusula* (a text about a method of effecting propitiation) which was composed by Guru; after having written these, they prepared a list of these selections.

This is the legendary history and prophecy of Lhaci Pemasal disclosed by Guru Rinpoche:

At that time, King Thrisong Detsan invited the Guru and the royal family to Chimphu.[3] There, while King was offering a hundred and eight *ganacakras,*[4] his eight year old daughter Lhachi Pemasal, by the excellent queen Droza Jangchubmen ('bro boa' baying hub sman), died. The King looked at the dead princess. His face was bathed in tears and he fainted. Yeshe Tshogyal took off her white silk head scarf and, after she scattered sandal wood water, the king regained his senses. Then the Guru consoled the King as follows:

O King, the activity of the world is like a dream.
The essential characteristic of a compound is but an illusion.
The Kingdom is like a yesterday's dream.
The public wealth is like a dew drop.
Impermanent life is like a bubble of water.
What is compound is precarious and perishes.
Man's life ends in death. Union ends in separation.
So it is with all aggregates on the earth.
There is nothing permanent, stable.
Without holding impermanent as permanent.
Cultivate the unoriginated Dharmakaya.

Then the King, wincing with a painful scowl, arose and presented the Guru with a golden cup full of turquoises. Bowing down to him, he said, "Oh! you, are a great Master and Bearer of Knowledge!" If the essential characteristic of compound is impermanence, when will my monastery be ruined? when will decline the teaching of the Buddha Dharma take place? What will be the cause of its decline or disappearance? What is the cause and effect of her premature death? What bond have I broken with regard to my child? In the future, where will she takes rebirth? Finally, will the time of the Celestial Awakening come to her or not? I am asking the great Master, the Jewel, to speak."
The Master said, "Lord King, listen:

"In this monastery, which you have built, there will come forth many proprietors who will be the causes of its ruin. Do not lament over their sacrileges! All is subject to decay. In the Ox Year of sixty one, King, you will pass away.

After that the Mongolian will govern the laws of your Kingdom. At the end, the Chinese Government will capture power. Although the Buddha Dharma will flourish for many years, there will also be many ups and downs. In the time of the fifth Royal descendent after you, the Dharma of Holy Buddha will become corrupted and it will deteriorate. Householders will fill the monasteries and there will be fighting before the altar; the temples will be used as slaughter houses; the ascetics of the caves will return to the cultivated valleys, and the yogis will become traders;[5] thieves will own wealth and cattle; monks will become householders while priests and spiritual leaders will turn to robbery, brigandage and thievery. Corrupt and selfish men will become leaders while abbots will turn into army officers to lead their monks as soldiers; nuns will put their own bastards to death. Sons will see their estates and inheritances stolen from them. Mean and vulgar demagogues will become local leaders, while young girls will instruct the youth in the schools. The scriptures of the *Tathagatas*,[6] the images of the Buddha, the sacred icons, the scroll paintings and the Stupas will be desecrated, stolen and bartered at the market price; their real worth will be forgotten. When religious duties will be forgotten, spirits of darkness, which had been controlled by ritual power, will become unloosed and frenzied and will control the mind of whatever being they possess. Spirits with vindictive power will possess monks; spirits of egoistic wickedness will possess the *Mantradhara* or magicians; grasping, quarreling spirits will possess women; every man, woman and child in the country will be possessed by uncontrollable forces of darkness. The signs of these times will be new and fantastic modes of dress traditional styles will be forgotten; the monks will wear fancy robes and the nuns will dress before a mirror. Every man will have to carry a weapon to protect himself and each man will have to guard his food from poison. The Abbots and Masters will poison their pupils' minds and hearts; the executive and the legislature will disagree; men will become lewd and licentious; and women will become licentious and unchaste; monks will ignore their discipline and moral code; the *Mantradharas* will break their Covenant. The good ways of behaving will whirl away like snatches of fog and the bad ones will arise like whirlwinds. The Royal Dharma will become last night's dream. The precious ones, the *Three Jewels*, will be abandoned by all like the dead, and those dear to each one, fathers and mothers, will be thrown on the points of spikes. When people have done evil, they will say, The Time is bad'.

"The Celestial Order, disrupted, will loosen plague, famine and war to terrorize terrestrial life. No rain will fall in season, only out of season; the valleys will be flooded. Famine, frost and hail will give many unproductive years. The rapacious female demons *(mamo)* and the twelve guardian protectors of the Dharma, unpropitiated and enraged, will release diseases, horrible epidemics and plagues which will spread like wildfire, striking men and cattle. Earthquakes will bring sudden floods while fire, storms and tornadoes will destroy temples, stupas and cities in an instant. The Muslim Turks will conquer India; the Garlok army will suppress the Dharma in Kashmir; the Mongols will conquer Tibet; the Jang army will enter Kham. The protector's Temple, Rasa Thral Nang (ra sa 'phral snang), in Lhasa, will be threatened; the famous temple of Samye will desecrated; the King's law will broken and the strength of communal unity will be lost. The passes, valleys and narrow paths will be terrorized by shameless brigands; fearful, lawless and leaderless people will fight with one another; each man will work selfishly. Tibet will become corrupted and defiled. At that time, most fortunate people and Dharma practitioners will run away from Tibet. Even you, the king, should hide your books because in future they will be of great use. *Sutras* having become meaningless talk, only a few may attain liberation, depending on themselves. Yet the teaching of the *Terma* will not confused; it will be a great benefit. The door of Treasure having been opened by many fortunates and *Tertons*, the Buddha Dharma will flourish again."

Again, the Lord King, bowing down to him, asked, "O Great Guru, what will be the cause of such an event? In which year will it occur? When will it end? Please tell us the means to prevent the coming disaster."

The Great Guru replied, "Listen well, O great King, the answer to your question is this:

"Once upon a time, when the Lord Buddha was challenged by powerful demons, they were defeated totally. At that time, the Demons prayed that at the end of the Religion of Buddha all should become their subjects. It will be a time when almost all the people will be confused and will do only evil. The masters of the High Tantras will stray like dogs in the streets and their faithless, errant students will roam like lions in the jungles. Embodiments of malice and selfishness will become revered teachers, while the achievements of Tantric Adepts will be reviled and the guidance of the secret guru execrated; the precepts of the Buddha are ignored and the advice of yogis and sages unsought. Robes will become uniforms worn by fools and villains while monks will wear foreign dress; even murderers will wear sacred robes. Men will resort to maledictory enchantments, learning *Mantras* for selfish ends; monks will prepare potions to blackmail, extort and gain profit. All good customs and habits will be rejected and many despicable innovations corrupt; following errant paths, men will be trapped by their own mean actions; the avaricious and spurious protectors of the pure teachings will no longer fulfill their functions.

"At this time the Mongolian army will occupy Tibet. They will head for battle in the Iron Dog Year. The battle will take place in the Water Horse Year. There will be great ferocity in the Fire Ox Year. In the Wood Sheep Year, peace will prevail for some time.

"All this can be avoided by maintaining good law in the Kingdom. Abandon all evils in the way of Governing Kingdom. Perform the ten virtuous acts and encourage the practitioners to follow strictly the discipline of *Vinaya* and *Mantra;*[8] having renovated the monasteries that deteriorate, recite the Dharma; having renovated the Stupas, supppress the Earth enemy; do not throw out the wealth treasure and do not even dig Earth treasure; having performed the practice of the wrathful deity, tame the *Masing* (*ma-sring)* to do good activities; having offered the religious service, please the Gods and Demons by *Kangdo (bskang mdos)* offering.[9] If this is done, it may help to prevent the evil for some time. It will not be totally prevented, because it is the *Karma* of masses. After five hundred years during which the people have done evil, they will say, 'The time is bad. There was no day in the village of Tibet, it moved like a fragrant grass. There was no leisure in life, it was like a shooting star. The good was replaced by the bad.' At that time, the foreign forces will conquer the Tibet. Men will perish like flies in the springtime. Possessions being ownerless, the markets will be like houses at festival time." The King, in despair, was weeping abundantly.

The Master said, "It is the *Karma* of beings, Do not weep! O King, the cause of making untimely death of your princess was this:

བྱ་རུང་ཁ་ཤོར།

"Before this life, she was the queen of King Bhilakutra, in the town of Kamasrita in the east of India. She was the King's first wife, but she had no son; the second wife had one son. Being jealous of the boy, the first queen killed him, and it is the fulfillment of this deed which has cut off her life prematurely. In this life father and daughter are brought together. Now, in the existence before the last one, in Nepal, I myself, Padma, you the Lord King, and the Bodhisattva, were three brothers. At the Stupa of Maguta, near *Svayambhucaitya,* we attached a Kolasa, and each one made a vow. At that time the princess was a wasp, and she stung you in the vein of your neck. Without paying attention, you rubbed your neck with your hand and the wasp died; you had so much regret and pity for it that, with fervor, you made a vow in your mind: 'May later, in a thousand years, ...'" The Master was silent for some time and then said, "If I explain these things, the heart of the King will suffer."

The King said, "The price does not matter. Speak, I beg you!" So, Padma continued: "As the King wishes.

"This princess Lotus, seven births earlier in India, was born in the monastery of Kotala as Jatala, a child of a Brahman. Having become a Monk (*bhiksu*), this son was earning his living by reciting the texts; he recited a hundred books of the King of Kotala, and, after many days, one evening the King gained belief in the Dharma. Now the bhiksu went out to purify his body. Seeing some dogs who were copulating in a flower garden, he was seized with desire, and returning to the palace and embracing the queen, he broke the moral rule. While the Monk was throwing dirt into the face of the dharma, the King, with his two eyes, observed his holy priest."Bad times"he said : 'That such men become Monk. The Monk developed a hatred for the dog and hit him on the penis with a rice beater . The dog died, and the people cursed the bhiksu who, after coming to his senses, threw himself from the roof of the palace. Being reborn five hundred times a female quadruped.... O pity .... she wiped out innumerable tribulations. Having sold stolen oil in a monastery, she had five hundred existences as a Ghost..... which alternated with five hundred births in hell. Having bullied a commentator of the Dharma, she took up a hundred existences as a titan. Having offered flowers and made the ritual tour of the monastery, she took on a hundred divine births. Again because of the remaining Karma of earlier births, she was born seven times as a dog at Samye itself. After that she was born three generations as ugly and unfortunate girls. Finally having encountered me [pedma] and by my blessing her, her evil Karma were purified and she born as a fortunate being and attained Buddhahood."

This was the prophecy made to the King on the occasion of the premature death of his daughter Lhachi Pemasal.

Again, the Lord King, bowing down to him, asked, "When will she be born as a human being? What Dharma will she embrace? When will she be able to free herself from this cyclic existence? Where will she perform acts of welfare for all sentient beings?"

གུ་རུ་ཆོས་དབང་།

"O King, listen and give me your full attention. At Yarlung,[10] she will be born as a girl of ugly body and meager luck, and she will have ten existences as a beggar. Then, transmigrating to Layag in the South-West, in the year of the monkey, she will be born as a young woman gifted with wisdom. As soon as she is born, her father and mother will die, though she will later meet me, incarnated as Nyang Ral and, showing me respect, she will seize the right path. Then, in Tsang, in the Yeru (gyas ru) district, in the Red Village, she will be born as the son of contemplative Buddhist parents. This son will be of ugly countenance and will snarl reproaches, and, in religious habit, will be an arch-heretic. But meeting me, incarnated as Chowang (chos dbang), he will be able, on my advice, to see the essence of knowledge, and the dakinis will make him welcome. Transmigrating from this existence, next in the plain of Drin ('brin thang) at the border of Do (Tibet), and mon (Bhutan), she will be born as the son of esteemed and noble parents, in the year of Iron Female Hare. This son will be different, of fine figure, of pure senses, and wise. Yet he will become an orphan, indigent and unhappy, the butt of the hostility of all his relatives. Now, with the tendencies of his previous life, he will enter the monkhood.

"In the Water Ox Year, he will find my profound treasure. Three doors of it will be opened, but even at that time, although he will have an opportunity to meet with the instruction of the *Heart-drop*, there won't be much benefit for the welfare of others. However, as it will be the time of practicing the Hidden Way, at that time will appear seventy fortunate and unfortunate students who will embrace my profound teaching. Those who have accumulated evil Karma will take birth in lower realms. At that time, as prophesied by the Dakinis, will appear twenty good disciples. Especially the possessor of the treasure of the profound mysticm of *Heart-drop* will appear to a Monkey Year girl of Drak Zungkhar (sgrags zung mkhar), who is very beautiful, possessing great wisdom and faith in the Dharma and has been repeatedly blessed by Dakini Yeshe Tshogyai. If the instructions are given to her, she would attain Buddhahood in the upper region of the sloping valley of Kharak and the Dharma may have flourished for a while. If not, most of the people will become evil minded and there won't be much help for sentient beings, and only few will keep faith in it. Whosoever happens to meet him, will be blessed and will follow the path of liberation. His life span will fifty nine years. But if he practices the propitiatory ritual of life for longevity, he may live till fifty nine years, otherwise, there are chances of his dying earlier because of some impediments. Confess your guilt for what your disciples have done, i.e., those who have broken the vows. For this you have to repent to purify the vows; if you do so you will live for fifty nine years. At that time a girl will appear through the blessing of a group of five *Dakinis (mkha' 'gro sde long)* and by her mystical rites and activities you may live even longer than the years given above.

"At that time the profound treasures will be taken away from Tibet to lower plain of Bumthang (bumthang smad) in Bhutan. If you (lama) fail to take them away to Bumthang, hide them in the same place where they were discovered or hide them in such a place where Gods and Demons don't pass or exist, so that they may appear in future.

"Having passed from this life, Pema Ledreltshal (padma las bral tshal) will enter into the *Sambhogakaya* realm for a little while as Kunkhen Longchen Rabjampa (kun mkhyen klong chen rab byams pa). Meanwhile, Pema Lingpa (padma glingpa), having born at Bumthang Tharpaling in the Kingdom of Bhutan, at the age of fifteen will open the treasure door of *Heart drop (Nyingthig)* in the lion-like rock at the lower plain of Bumthang and will serve all sentient beings. Thereafter, having opened many treasure doors and performed various miracles, the five Dakinis who took the form of girls having become her mother, will do incalculable good to all beings. Having been known as Drimed 'Odzer, a son named Dawa Drakpa, the incarnation of Tandin (rta mgrin), will be born. There will also be hundred and eight students who will have realized the path of religion of *Dzogchen Nyingthig*. There will be thirty disciples who will successfully fulfill the purpose of sentient beings. There will be many patrons and supporters of him. He will establish and develop Dzogchen teaching at Lhodrak Kharchu (lho brag mkhar chu) At that time all kinds of *mind section (sems sde)* will appear from the face of Lhodrak Senge. From Monkhar

Teng (mon-mkhar-steng) my profound *guidance section (man sngas sde)* will emerge.

"Her things which are hidden at Chimphu are: Silk robe (zab ber srubs med), Turquoise of purple color (gyu gung ri kha dmar), precious stone or Gem which is believed to have the property of curing paralysis (gzi mchong spel ma'i lan tsha), a mirror of silver, a robe of Golden parrot (chos gos gser gi ha ri) of Guru Rinpoche, and a skull filled with the Tantric instructions of four empowerments which could liberate one in this life itself etc. These will appear at the time of her next life when she takes birth in Bumthang. Revealing those treasures he will do incalculable good to beings. In that birth, having attainded Buddhahood, she will serve all sentient beings from the *Sambhogakaya* and will not take birth anymore.

"Then we, you the Lord King, Yeshe Tshogyal, Lhacam and I, Padma, will meet in the prosperous copper-colored mountain of (zang dog dpal ri)."[11]

The King was delighted and, after having made countless obeisances and circumambulations, he again requested of Padmasambhava, the second Buddha: "Since there is no essence in the Samsaric activities. Please give me instructions which will liberate me permanently into Buddhahood, which is comfortable and peaceful, here and hereafter." Guru Rinpoche proclaimed :

> *Eh ma ho (Wonderful!) O great King listen again.*
> *Since there is no essence in the Samsaric (worldly) Dharma.*
> *Having wandered without limitation, you have to suffer again and again in Samsara.*
> *Therefore, rule the Kingdom according to Dharma.*

Do remember that the unoriginated Dharmadhatu is as an essence of the Kingdom.
Adhere to the forest of solitude as an essence of place.
Look for luminous empty nature as an essence of monastery.
Take your innate mind as an essence of house.
Hold by the remembrance of consciousness as an essence of an entire habitation.
Generate the Bodhi mind as an essence of store-room.
Depend on two merits as an essence of wealth.
Endeavor to practice the ten virtuous acts as an essence of Business.
Bear the sentient beings with commpassion as an essence of father.
Preserve the pristine nature of emptiness as an essence of mother.
Adhere to inseparable development and the completive phase as an essence of Son.
Comprehend the bde-gsal mi-rtog (kind of meditation) as an essence of wife.
Look for the teachings of Buddha as an essence of friend.
Generate unflagging faith as an essence of sphere or field.
Eat unoriginated ambrosial food as an essence of nourishment.
Drink the nectar of religious advice as an essence of thirst.
Wear modesty and shame as an essence of dress.
Depend on tantric deities like Ma sring, dam can etc. as an essence of attendant.
Carry on religious activity as an essence of enjoyment

Look for one's own mind as an essence of entertainment.
Do meritorious activities as an essence of the bustle of worldly affairs.
Contemplate the completive phase as an essence of Vacillation.
Depend on precept and empowerment as an essence of relatives.
Improve the five moral poisons as an essence of passionate attachment.
Adhere to impartial thought and understanding as an essence of ornaments.
Write profound holy book as an essence of work.
Take impartial alms as an essence of guest.
Turn one's innermost heart to Dharma as an essence of Council.
Workship the Triple Gems as an object to which offerings are made (mchod gnas).
Honor humbly one's parents as an essence of reverence.
Adhere to Vajra Guru as an essence of benediction.
Act without pretext mind as an essence of precepts.
Abandon all sufferings as an essence of obligation.
Adhere to the pure three vows as an essence of monastery rather than a Lord's house.
Look for unchangeable celestial emptiness as an essence of Mandala.
Tame one's own temperament as an essence of Instruction.
Look for unchangeable celestial emptiness as an essence of contemplation.
Keep one's mind as it is (i.e. in natural state) as an essence of meditation.

Examine the error of dualism as an essence of perpetrated deed.
Accomplish by the miraculous an essence of result.

"If you, the Lord, do likewise, you will be happy and comfortable here and hereafter and shortly you will obtain Buddhahood."

The King was delighted and made serene again, and did countless obeisances and circumambulations.

This was the advice given to the Lord King by Padmasambhava.

Thereafter, having put the Lhacam's silk dress etc., in the maroon colored leather-box, hidden it as the treasure, and having prayed that all this should be found by Lhacam in her next life, the Guru then wrote a Ni (ཉི) with the red ink of wisdom, and having drawn back her consciousness, she was able to breath and speak. After that she was initiated (abhiseka) into the empowerment of *Heart drop (Nyingthig)* teachings and given an esoteric name, Pedma Ledreltshal.[12] She put the *'Holy Books'* Box on her forehead and prayed to find this casket in future and to be able to do beneficial service to all sentient beings.

The Guru Rinpoche said to Lhacam, "When you will awaken from the defilement of the Karma of your previous lives, we, the Lord King, you, Lhacam and I, Pedma, will meet." Again, her consciousness passed away. Having demonstrated the manner of burning the death body itself, Guru Rinpoche took it at once to Uddiyana and performed sacrificial offerings to purify her defilement. Again he came back immediately and told Yeshe Tshogyal to record all these events and hide the record together with profound treasure, so that in future when she comes across it, she will be moved by great faith and devotion.

This will give Lhacam a strong aspiration to benefit sentient beings after being empowered and blessed by the Guru Padmasambhava. Thereafter, Yeshe Tshogyal requested Guru Pedma whether this advice about the esoteric teaching of *Heart drop* was to be propagated or hidden. The Guru replied, "It is not the right time to propagate it. So it is necessary to hide it as treasure." Having placed the *Box of the Holy Text* of Lhacam on her head, and prayed that it would be her dharma fate [to propagate these teachings] in her incarnation.

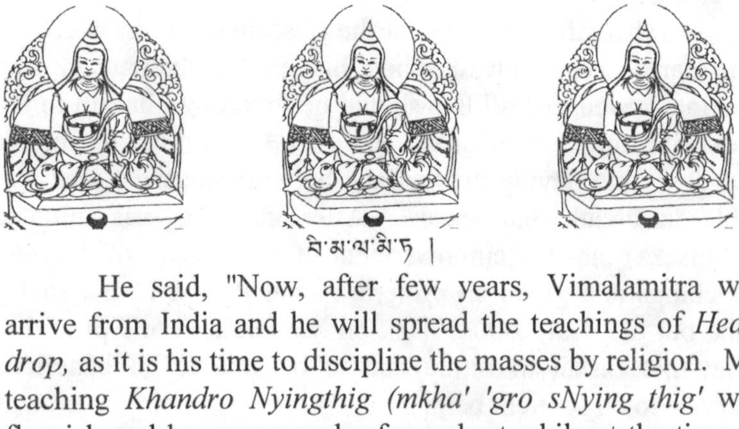

བི་མ་ལ་མི་ཏྲ །

He said, "Now, after few years, Vimalamitra will arrive from India and he will spread the teachings of *Heart drop,* as it is his time to discipline the masses by religion. My teaching *Khandro Nyingthig (mkha' 'gro sNying thig'* will flourish and become popular for a short while at the time of the decline of the former *Heart drop.* This too, generally the those [teachings], development of Nyingma (rnying ma) tradition will be short. Among the doctrine of the *Terma's (gter ma)* development and the opening of the *Terma* door will take place simultaneously; Since there are no more fortunate possessors of the treasure, most of them will diminish. So, it is good to hide it." A set of *'Kusula'* (a text about meditational processes) was hidden at Dagpo(dags po) and Lung Thramo (lung khra-mo). At lower Bumthang, in a lion-like rock, he hid a treasure of reflection, together with

Tantras, Mantras, Sastras, the Kangyur (dkar 'gyur),[13] *the Tengyur (brtan 'gyur),*[14] *the Ju Bum (rGyud-'bum) and Gur bum (mgur-'bum), the hundred thousand Agamas, the Drub Bum (sgrub'bum), the Zung Bum (gzungs-'bum) and the Ngag Bum (sngags-'bum),* and more, and he entrusted them to the Dakinis of the treasure owners, *Mamos,* and Za (*gza*). And he made exhortation to hand over those treasures to the fortunate ones when the life span of people will decline to fifty years.

This is all about an entrustment of treasures to Lhacam and the ḍākiṇis and others by the great Guru.

At that time, five very profound Terma treasures were hidden. They were those out of one hundred and eight treasures that were hidden in Tibet and Bhutan by Guru Padmasambhava:

1. In the Centre of Tibet, Zhithro Kedzog (zhi khro bskyed rdzogs), the generative and completive phase of peaceful, wrathful and heart treasures that were hidden at Chimphu as the treasure of Body.

2. In the South of Tibet, at Khachu (mkhar chu), he hid the full perfection, such as Desheg Duspa (bde gshegs 'dus pa) etc., as the treasure of knowledge. Medicine, astrology etc. were not included in the knowledge treasures, since they are ordinary or common.

3. In the Western Tibet, the master hid a set of the profound doctrines of Dakas and Dakinis at Lharing Drak (lha ring brag) as the treasure of speech.

4. In the Western Tibet, he hid a Yangphu Taphak (yang phur rta phag)etc., at Zangyak Kha Dzong (zang yang

nam mkha' rdzong) and Tidro Drak (ti sgro brag), as the treasure of work or activity.

5. In the eastern Tibet he hid Zhichok gi Drupa Ngonsum 'Odsal dampa Yeshe Tshowor Gyurpa Khandro Nyingthig (zhi mchog gi sgrub pa mnon sum 'od gsal gyi gdams pa ye shes gtso boor gyur pa mkha 'gro sNyingthig) and other Terma at Lungthrmo Drak (lung khra mo brag) and Bumthang as the treasure of mind. This was an enumeration of the Yangter (yang gter) treasures hidden at that time.

This, in brief, is the conclusion of the supplication made at the beginning.

NOTES

1 Theg pa dgu, (yanas),the nine vehicles are: (1) Sravaka, (2) Pratyekabuddha, (3) Bodhisattva, (4) Kriyayoga-tantra, (5) Upayoga-tantra, (6) Yoga-tantra, (7) Mahayoga tantra, (8) Anuyoga, (9) Atiyoga. 1-2 belong to the Hinayana or Lesser Vehicle; 3-9 are Mahayana or Great Vehicle path; 4-9 are Vajrayana or tantric paths; 4-6 are outer tantric Vehicles; 7-9 are divisions of the Anuttarayoga-tantra, the inner, supreme or ultimate tantra. This nine-fold division is a Nyingma formulation; the other school count only the first six.

2 *'Og Min, Akanistha*; the highest Nirmanakaya Buddha-field, but usually used to mean the highest Buddha realm, where absolute reality is perceived as a multi-dimensional phenomenal panorama.

3 *mChims phu*, the high part of mChims.

4 *Tshogs kyi 'khor lo*, Ganacakras; a feast offering; (1) a circle of devotees and or gods and goddesses assembled for an offering sacrament; (2) the essential, tantric sacramental rite of offering itself; (3) the accumulation of offerings for the sacrament. In the life it would appear that a feast, or even an ordinary meal, was transformed into a ganacakras rite; and when offerings were to be made it was always an occasion for a Ganacakras.

5 *rnal 'byor pa (Yogi*), literally, 'He who has attained perfect serenity,' but usually interpreted as an ascetic possessing magic powers.

6 *De bzhin gshegs pa,* (Tathagata; thus come or thus gone), another name for Buddha.

7 *mchod rten* (stupa); originally, a memorial mound containing the relics of the Buddha, symbolizing the mind of the Buddha, the Dharmakaya. Later, the relics of other enlightened beings, scriptures, statues, etc., were included in stupas. Stupas are objects of veneration and range from simple altar pieces to very large structures which may be seen for miles around.

8 *dge ba bcu*; abstention from killing, stealing, sexual misconduct (body); lying, slander, calumny and cursing (speech); and covetousness, malice and opinionatedness (mind)

'Dul ba (Vinaya); that portion of the Buddhist canon that deals with monastic discipline and ethics in general. Also see Tharthang Tulku, Crystal Mirror Vol. V , p. 36.

sngags, Mantra; is explained in the tantras as that which protects the cohesiveness of the Vajra mind. It is a means of transforming energy through sound, expressed by speech, breathing, and movement. Mantra is always done in conjunction with visualization and mudra, in accordance with the prescription of a Sadhana transmitted by one's guru.

9 See G.Tucci, The Religion of Tibet, pp,176-183.

10 *Yarlung;* a river valley in central Tibet, the cradle of Tibetan civilization.

11 *Zangs mdog dpal ri*; Guru Padma's paradise, afterwards created on the south western island continents of nga yab gling.

12 *dbang skur (abhiseka)*; a sprinkling, empowerment, or initiation : A ceremony in which a student is ritually entered into a mandala of a particular tantric deity by his Vajra master. He is thus empowered to practice the Sadhana of that deity. In anuttarayogayana there are four principal abhisekas: (1) vase abhiseka which includes the abhisekas of the five Buddha families : Water (Vajra), crown (Ratna), vajra (padma), bell (karma), and name (Buddha); (2) secret abhiseka ; (3) Prajnajnana-abhiseka; and (4) fourth abhiseka.

13 The *bka' 'gyur* contains the texts revealed by the Buddha, including texts on discipline, metaphysics, various teachings, the Tantras, etc.

14 The *bstan 'gyur* contains the treatises and the various commentaries on Buddha's teachings that have been translated from Sanskrit into Tibetan.

BOTH IN THIS WORLD AND THE NEXT
DESIRES GIVE RISE TO GREAT MISFORTUNE;
IN THIS LIFE KILLING, BONDAGE AND FLAYING,
AND IN THE NEXT THE EXISTENCE OF THE HELLS.
SHANTIDEVA

CHAPTER TWO

AN ACCOUNT OF TRULKU PEMA LEDREL-TSAL AND THE REVEALATION OF THE TREASURE 'KHANDRO NYINGTHIG'

ཆོས་ལོངས་སྤྲུལ་གསུམ།

The various prophecies were made by Guru Rinpoche in connection to Lhaci Pemasal.[1] In this chapter, we will focus on the life of and the revelation of *Khandro Nyingthig* by Trulku (sprul sku) Pema Ledreltsal,[2] the incarnation of Lhachi Pedmasal.

Lhaci Pemasal was born at Yarlung three times in succession as a poor girl. After that, she was born as a blind bitch-dog at the village of Rolkaru in Yarlung. Having been chopped to death, she was reborn as a bird, Rig Kang Kang (rigs rkang rkang). Then, transmigrating to the market of Lhasa, she was born as an ewe. These five "impure" lives having cleared away the evil karmas, the five 'pure' lives began with two existences as nuns.[3] In the centre of Drakda Drongsar (sgrags mda' grong gsar), having been born as a girl, she woke from her previous persona and renounced the householder's life and became a nun. She went to Samye monastery and, while she was circumambulating, the rebirth of King Songtsan took place at Lhodrak Tamshul (lho brag gtan shul); he was named Nyang Ralpa or Nyang Nima Odzer (myang ral pa or myang nyima 'od-zer, 1124-1192 or 1136-1204). The Trulku revealed the profound heart treasure from Sinmo Barje Drak (srin mo sbar rjes brag). The spiritual son of Ugyen Rinpoche, he became a master of Tantra and Mantrayana. The right time had arrived to reveal the profound treasure from Samye Jangchub Ling (samyes byang chub gling). So they, the Guru and his disciples, arrived at Samye. While revealing the profound treasures gradually, he saw a nun possessing good qualities and, he took her with him to Tamshul (gtam shul) and made her an esoteric consort. She, after having been given an instructions, realised the essence of nature and was also named Rigma Sangay Kyi (rig ma sangs rgyas skyid).

After that, in the Monkey Year, a beautiful girl, gifted with wisdom, was born to a rich father named Tshurpa Sangay Pema (tshur pa sangs rgyas padma), who lived toward the south-east country of Layak, at the lower village of Za (rza) and he was given the name Pema Drolma (padma sgrol ma). At that time, Chowang Rinpoche (1212-73) the incarnation of King Thrisong Detsan, was born at a village called Pang Drong (spang grong). After having revealed treasure from Namkay Chan (gnam skas can) and Drakmo Thrang (brag mo phreng), etc., and also from many treasure places, he became a master of Vajrayana. In the course of time, he came across Pema Drolma and, having seen her as a fortunate and gifted girl, he took her as a consort. They had three children, only two whom survived Sangay Kundral (sangs rgyas kun grol) (daughter) and Pema Wangchen (padma dbang chen) (son). Having been instructed by their father, both of them realized the profound knowledge of the essence of Dharma. Having thought of propagating the religion, they built the famous Guru Temple, at the cost of a great deal of hardship, in the Lhodrak province of Tibet. They felt it necessary to send Pema Wangchen as a 'hostage' to secure wood from the Sub-Himalayan regions of Bhutan.[4]

ཉང་རལ་ཉི་མ་འོད་ཟེར།

The next embodiment was one Rinchen Drak (rin chen grags), a hereditary trantric priest from Drongsar valley in the Tsang province of Tibet. At that time, he had an opportunity to meet Terton Ugyen Lingpa (1329-67). Upon request, he bestowed the completed teachings or instructions about tuterly deity called Tandin Chag Ralchan (rta mgrin lcags ral can). Having endeavoured to perform this Sadhana and followed it, he was able to meet the Terton five times. By practicing other instructions, he made a minute examination of his own mind and so came to understand the profound meaning of the nature of mind itself. Then transmigrating to Drinthang (brin thang) south of the Loro and Nyal (gnyal) districts of South-East Tibet, he was born to a tantric priest and his sister in the year of the Iron Hare (1291-1316) and was given the name Pema Ledreltshal.[5] Since his parents were weak and poor, they were very much disliked by their neighbours. One day when he was at Drinthang Koro, he met an elderly monk. He questioned him, "where are you going, *Geshe* ?"[6] The elderly monk replied, saying, "I am not going anywhere but to your place." Then, suddenly, he took out a scroll of paper from his breast pocket and gave it to him. He said, "son, look carefully at this scroll of paper and according to each word and without error, reveal it. There is your share of spiritual power (dngos grub)." Saying this, the monk vanished.

Having returned to his hometown, one day he read the scroll paper. It said that "the coming Water Ox Year is the right time to reveal your treasure shared (chos skal). Go on the 10th of Tonda Rava (i.e. from the middle of August to the middle of September). On the side of the cliff of the Dagpo'i Danglung Thramo (dags po'i dang lung khra mo) there is a figure of (Svastika, gyung drung) the mystic cross (卐), written with red ink. To the East and West of it, there are stone dices weighing about one and half kilograms. While you dig at that spot, the profound treasured will appear." As the letter instructed, Pema Ledreltshal went to Danglung and stayed three days at the Cave of Kharmo and revealed all the treasures during those days. While returning, he arrived at upper Nyal and, having gone to Sho Tsherma Lung (sho tser ma lung), he stayed at the house of a tantric priest. They offered him delicious food and, as in Tibetan custom, they gave him a lots of local made wine (usually served after dinner). In the night after having conversed a lot, a priest suddenly asked him. "Where have you come from and what is your purpose?" Pema Ledreltshal said, "Because of previous prophecy, I have been to Dangspo to take out the treasures." The Tantika said, "Have you got the profound treasures?" "Yes, I have got them," said Pema. "Well, what are they?" "They are the *Heart drop of Dakinis*, the instruction Nenpo Lhasum (gnen po lha gsum), Tantara and the Sadhana of Zadu (gzah bdud)." "If so, you should bless us with that box of holy texts." He blessed all the family members with the box. The next day, early in the morning, he set out on the journey to his hometown, and the son of the Tantika, named Legpa Gyaltshen (leg pa rgyal mtshan), followed him. They arrived at Drinthang safely. At that time, the public of Drinthang started saying, with one voice, that he is neither from a Tantikas' lineage, nor does he possess knowledge of it. So, how could he reveal the treasures, and what treasure has been revealed?" He was accused by his neighbours of perpetrating fraud. When he came to know about it, he felt sorry for the people of his village. So, he decided to wander into Tibet, accompanied by his disciples Legpa Gyaltshen, Namkha Wangchuk; Rindor and Palye. They set off on their directionless journey. They arrived at Yarlung by way of Jar (byar) and Ae. They made a three day pilgrimage to Sheldrak. Then they left for Samye and visited to all its temples. From there, they went to Chimphu and decided to make a pilgrimage for seven days, but on the fifth day, at midnight Pema Ledreltshal had a vision of the goddess Vajravarahi (rdo rje phag mo), who commanded him to go to Lhasa. "There you will meet your karmically-bound disciple," said the goddess. The next morning the five of them left for Lhasa. While circumambulating on the fifth day, the third Karmapa, Rangjung Dorje (rang byung rdo rje, 1284 - 1339), who was staying in a camp at Lhasa Ku Bumthang, said, "You, the master and disciples of the treasurer of Lhorong, come to my place!" Having arrived there, they bowed down and made an offering to him of a piece of flesh of the seventh incarnation of Brahmin,[7] a scarf and a set of musk. He asked, "Have you got any treasure text which you revealed? If so, then show it to me." The Lama (Pema Ledreltshal) explained that he only had the original *'yellow pages' (shog ser)* of the texts, since he had had no time to copy them out. The Karmapa was delighted and took their blessing on his head. That night the Karmapa dreamed that a red lady wearing bone ornaments informed him that Pema Ledreltshal, the spiritual son of Padmasambhava, possessed thc profound

ཀརྨ་པ་རང་བྱུང་རྡོ་རྗེ།

teachings of Vajrayana. "Request him to give the teachings of Vajrayana." The next day he sent a messenger to call him. Having arrived in his presence, the Karmapa said, "you should give me the initiation of yesterday's '*yellow pages.*'" He said, "You are a high lama and it may not be appropriate for me to give you such an initiation." But there was the strong order that he should impart the teachings by any means. So, not disrespecting his order, he gave the verbal authorization of the yellow pages that contained the teaching of *"the Heart drops of the Dakinis"* completely. Thus, he became the guru of the Karmapa too. After that, he returned to Drinthang Korodrak and made a seven-month retreat. At that time, he gave the complete teachings and verbal authorization to Legpa Gyaltshen. Again, he went into a three-month meditation retreat in front of Chorten Drak (mchod rten brag). Legpa Gyaltshen, who was staying in the lower region of Chorten Drak, met Rinchen Lingpa, who came to pay respect to Trulku Pema Ledreltsal. Since the Lama was in retreat, he was unable to meet him. So he requested Legpa Gyaltshen to instruct him in whatever teachings he had received from Trulku. He gave him the complete initiation and empowerment of the *Heart drop of Dakini.* The Trulku, after having completed his retreat, left to the lower region of the Nyal district; at the foot of Nyalmed Serchen Bum (gnal smad ser chen 'bum) he met Legspa

Gyaltshan and Rinchen Lingpa, who were coming to see him. The saint asked, "Where are you two going?" "We are coming to see you." "If so, come let us go to Drinthang," said he. And they proceeded to Drinthang. There they stayed in Choling monastery and disclosed to Rinchen Lingpa that in China, "There is a treasure at Kha'i Phawang Rubal Nagpo (Kha'i pha dbang rus sbal nag po). Therefore, take these papers and reveal those treasures and do good for all sentient beings." At that time he was twenty five, and it was 'Lokag' (an inauspicious year) for him. From Nyal, they went up and reached Nyalmed Huru district, where they stayed in the corner of a dirty place. At that time, women came gathering, among whom was a lady who looked like the one who had been prophesied by the Guru. Thinking her to be the one, he requested her to allow them to spend a night in her house. She said, that is fine, but, first of all, tell me who you are and from where you are coming," Legpa Gyaltshen said, "We are from Drinthang. Have you not heard about a Trulku Pema Ledreltshal? He is with us". The lady felt happy and welcomed them into the house and rendered them good service for the duration of one month. For some time, he had also physical relations (gsang spyod) with her and told her to keep it a secret. That autumn, as usual, they departed for the seasonal alms round and reached Darma Khalung village near upper Nyal, where they stayed at Rindors' house. That very night, in a morning dream, there appeared a girl who said, "Listen you, son of Ugyen, the lady with whom you have practiced the rites of sexual yoga is in fact a demoness. The girl with whom you had a karmical relationship is to the west of this house. See her tomorrow." Having said this, she vanished. In the morning, he thought he should look for her, whether or not she was there. But to his surprise, he saw a beautiful girl with all good qualities. Good height, a white complexion, a sweet nature and mole like a lotus on her forehead. He greatly regretted his relationship with the previous lady. And he immediately wanted to have mystical [i.e., karmical] contact with the new lady. Having collected alms food gradually, they stored it in the house of Legpa Gyaltshan and went to their host's house with empty hands. The lady of lower Nyal asked them, "Where have you stored your alms? I have nourished the five of you for almost one month. Now, why didn't you bring your alms food here?" She scolded them. So they left her house with all their belongings. She, being a demoness, tricked her husband and brothers, telling them that the saint and his followers had stolen some of their belongings. They pursued the five and, at the border of Jar Ngo (Byar ngos), they were caught, all their properties were seized, and they were beaten badly. Rindor was killed, and her husband, jealous because of his wife, [tried to] hit Trulku with a knife but did not succeed. Hitting with a stone, he said, "I am an incarnation of the spiritual son of Ugyen Rinpoche. In fact, we did not steal any of your belongings. It is really too much to do such mischief to us. You will have to face the bad consequences of the *Triple Gems*. If you really wish to kill me, I will bring about my own death". Hearing this, the husband and brothers went away.

He and his disciples continued their journey and stayed in a small village called Julu Chung (gyu lu chung), behind a hill. That night Pema Ledreltsal said, "Legpa Gyaltshan and you three friends keep my 'treasure doctrines' (treasure-texts) without error. I will be born again to a father named Tenpa (bstan pa) and mother Sonam kyi (bsod nams skyid) in the centre of Gar Phuru in five years time. At that time, I will comprehend the present 'treasure-texts' and will benefit all sentient beings. At that time we will meet again," he said. Then, within five days, he disappeared into Dharmadhatu.[8]

NOTES

1 See chapter one.

2 The Heart-drop of the Dakinis, (mkha 'gro'i snying thig is the Dzongchen teaching that was given by Guru Rinpoche to King Thrisong Detsan's dying daughter, Lhacham Pema tsal (lha lcam padma rtsal) at Samye Chimphu. To console the king, Guru Rinpoche revived the princess and gave her these teachings after which she passed away. Guru Rinpoche also gave those teachings to Yeshe Tshogyal in the Great Gathering Cave of the Dakinis at Tidro in Drigung (the full name of which is gzho stod ti sgro brag dkar mkha' 'gro'i tshogs khang chen mo). The Khandro Nyingthig was hidden as terma at Dangla Thramo Drak in Dagpo (ldand lha khra mo brag) and revealed in 1253 by Pema Ledreltsal (1231-59), who was the reincarnation of Lhacham Pemasal.

3 BNPK., fo. 10b

4 Since Lhodrak Province of Tibet has scanty forest, GuruChowang had to send his only son as a 'hostage' to secure wood from the Sub-Himalayan region of Bhutan, while building the Guru Temple.

5 BNPK., fos. 11b-7a, RPZT. fos. 5a-6a.

6 Geshe (dge bshes), a high academic degree in Buddhist philosophy. Here it is used to as a polite form of addressing a elder.

7 The seven-rebirth pills (skye bdun ril bu) are prepared from sacred substances, originally including, it is said, the flesh of a person reborn seven successive lifetimes as a brahmin. The mere

taste of these is said to shut the doors of rebirth in the lower realms of Samsara.

8 Dharmadhatu (chos kyi dbyings), the absolute expanse: emptiness pervaded with awareness.

NOT TO DO ANY EVIL WHATSOEVER, TO CULTIVATE VIRTUE AND EVERYTHING ADMIRABLE, AND TO FULLY PURIFY ONE'S MIND THIS IS THE TEACHING OF BUDDHA.

DHAMMAPADA

CHAPTER THREE

KUNKHEN'S IMMENSE SERVICE TO LIVING BEINGS WHILE DWELLING IN THE SAMBHOGAKAYA REALM

Trulku Pema Ledreltsal, in order to accomplish his remaining tasks and duties, was reincarnated, just as he predicted before dying. He was known as Kunkhen in this new embodiment.

Kunkhen the 'all-knowing', 'all-understanding' Longchen Rabjampa (dri med 'od zer), known as the second Buddha, and certainly the greatest thinker in the Nyingma tradition (rnying ma pa), was born on the tenth day of the second month of the Earth Monkey Year of the fifth Rabjung (1308) at Teo Drong (stod grong) in Tra valley of Yuru Dra (gyo ru gra) province of central Tibet. He was a descendent, on his father's side, of the spiritual lineage of Rog Sherab 'Od (rog shes rab 'od), whose ancestry went back to Yeshe Wangpo Sung (ye shes dbang po srung), of the clan of Rog, who was one of the seven monks (sad mi bdun) ordained by Santaraksita around the year 790. He was also related to the clan of Gyalwa Chowang (rgyal ba mchog dbangs), one of

Padmasambhava's twenty-five foremost disciples, who gained mastery in the *Hayagriva Sadhana (pedma gsung)* and who was incarnated as Dusum Khenpa (dus gsum mkhyen pa, 1110-93), the greatest disciple of Gampopa (sgam po pa, 1079-1153). From his mother, Dromza Sonam Gyan ('brom gza ma bsod nams rgyan), he came from the ancestral lineage of Drom Tenpa ('Brom ston rgyal ba'i 'byung gnas, 1005-64), Atisa's foremost Tibetan disciple.

Like Buddha's mother, his mother too had an experience of wonder. In a dream, she saw a huge lion which, radiating light from his forehead that clearly illuminated the darkness of the three realm; it later entered her. As soon as he was born, he was nourished by the Dharma Protectors Namdo Rematí (nam gru re ma ti), who held the baby in her arms she said, "I will protect him;" she then handed him back to his mother and disappeared, in the same way as the Lord Indra did to Siddhartha, the Buddha. From childhood, he possessed the noble qualities of a Bodhisattva, including faith, compassion and wisdom. When he was five he learned to read and write with no difficulty. At seven, his father gave him initiations, instructions and training in the ritual performance of *The Peaceful and Wrathful Aspects of the Lama (lama zhi drak)* and in *Kagyad Dedus (bka' bgyad bde 'dus, revealed by Nyangral Nyima 'odzer), Phurpa* and *Tandin (rta mgrin).* At nine, he recited the *Nyithri (nyi khri)* and *Ja Tongpa (brgyad stong pa)* a hundred time. By then he had memorised the entire texts by heart and could recite them later on without reading them.

At twelve, Longchen Rabjampa received the ordination of renunciation at Samye, in the presence of the 'abbot' Khenpo Samdrup Rinchen (mkhan po bsam grub rin chen) and the Lama Kunga 'Odzer (Kun dga' 'od zer), at which time he was given the name Tshul Thrim Lodro (tshul thrim blo gros). Having practised the doctrine of the code of conduct (Vinaya) properly, he gained mastery of the Vinaya texts and taught them from the age of fourteen. At sixteen, he received empowerments, verbal authorisations and instruction from Tashi Rinchen (bkra shi rin chen) for the following texts: *Lam Dre (lam 'bras), Chodruk Nyi (chos drug gnyis), Phakmo Chodruk (phag mo chos drug), Dechok Drilbupa (bde mchog dril bu pa)* and *Chakdor Khorchen (phyag rdor 'khor chen)* and others. He also studied the *Jachod Naljor (bya spyod rnal 'byor), Dorje Thrangwa (rdo rje phreng ba), Dorje Gur (rdo rje gur), Khandro Gyatsho (mkha' 'gkro rgya mtsho), Sangay Thoepa (sangs rgyas thod pa)* and *Duski Khorlo (dus kyi 'khor lo*) etc., with the teachers Wang Ley (dbang les), Tentshul (ston tshul) and Throphuwa (khro phu ba). He listened many times to teachings about the instruction of the *Zhang Tshal, Go Tshangpa'i Lamthri (rgod tshang pa'i lam krid), Choyeil (gcod yul), Zhije Ngachir Barsum (zhi byed snga phyir bar gsum*) and others. from the Venerable Rinpoche Za lungpa and other personalities.

At nineteen, he joined an Institute of Sangphu Ne'u Thog (gsang phu ne'u thog) monastery, established by Lama Ngog Legpa'i Sherab (rngog legs pa'i she rab, the great logician. It was the only Institute of Logic in Tibet in those days. There he studied many works, including the five texts of *Jampa'i Cho Nga (byam pa'i chos lnga), the seven treatise on logic by Dharmakirti*, and numerous *Madhyamika* and *Prajna-Paramita* works, for six years, with Geshe Tsan Gonpo (btsan dgon po) and La Drangpa Chopel Gyaltshan (bla brang pa chos dpal rgyal mtshan), the successor of fifteenth and sixteenth abbots. He became more equipped and confident in the arts and sciences.

When he was in his late twenties, two events occurred which were to be of decisive importance to his intellectual and spiritual development. He had a vision of Padmasambhava and his Consort Yeshe Tshogyal, which resulted in his adopting the names of Drimed 'Odzer, given to him by Padmasambhava, and Dorje Zijid (rdo rje gzi brjid), conferred upon him by Yeshe Tshogyal, both in the vision. At this time (and one experience may well have lead to another), he became deeply attracted to, and involved in, the *Khandro Nyingthig,* mystical teachings connected with Padmasambhava, which he later developed in his own *Khandro Yangthig ('mkha' 'gro yang thig'.* From Wang Lodro Tenpa (dbang lo blo gros brtan pa), he studied *sutras,* the *Samadhiraja-Sutra, Prajnaparamita,* and *five other profound sutras*, the *commentary of 'Sherab Nyingpo, Buddhist philosophies, the science of words, Sanskrit, Poetics, Orthography (sdeb sbyor), Composition and drama, dramatic performance,* etc., and with that he was able to understand all other philosophical texts. While he was propitiating (sgrub pa mdzad pas) the God of wisdom, 'Manjushri, and other deities such as Tsho Denma (mtsho ldan ma), Mi Yowa (mi gyo ba), Phakar (Phag dkar), he had seen all their faces and was blessed by them, and especially by the Goddess of wisdom, 'Lhagpa'i Lha' Manjushiri, who

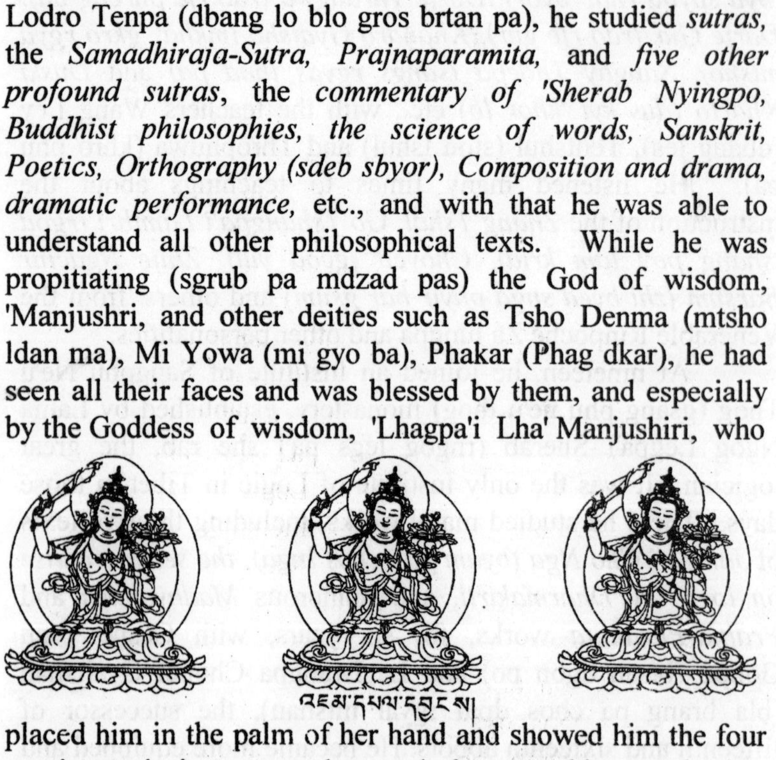

འཇམ་དཔལ་དབྱངས།

placed him in the palm of her hand and showed him the four continents in just seven days and also gave him prophecies. Because of the blessing of the God and Goddess of wisdom, he perfected his knowledge and became indisputable and unexaminable by other scholars. He had entirely defeated the non-Buddhist view. Almost all the scholars who came to debate with him were unable to speak when they were face to face with him. Because of his knowledge he became known by the title Sumlung Mangpo (bsam lung mang po) or Longchen Rabjampa (klong chen rab 'byams pa), which became popular not only in Samye but in all the directions of Tibet and abroad, and even in the land of spirits (mi ma yin gyi gnas).

Although he mastered various fields of learning and became extremely intellectual, he decided to follow the shortest path of liberation, like most noblemen or Bodhisattva (skyes bu chen po) did. Having travelled far and near, he was moved by the path of Bodhisattva Taktu Ngu's (rtag tu ngu) liberation.[1] Having learned Sutras, Tantras and Instructions many times from Lamas and spiritual friends, he increased his intellect by listening and thought. He abandoned partiality to any of the existing religious traditions of Tibet and simply acted like a bee which took the essence of many flowers. Later, he expounded the *Doju Semsum (mdo sgyu sems gsum), Nyingma Jubum (rnying ma rgyud 'bum)* and many other texts to four lamas, namely: (1) Denbakpa (dan bag pa), (2) Shenu Dendrup (gzhon nu don grub), (3) Nyothing Mawa (myos mthing ma ba), and (4) Sangay Drak (sangs rgyas grags), and at that time there also appeared the auspicious sign of oneness in the practice of Vajrayana. He wrote a Tika (commentary) called *Chokcheu Munsal Nyida Tingi Nangwa (phyog bcu mun sel nyi zl'i sprin gi snang ba)* on the essence of outer Tantra, in accordance with the *Heart drop Nyingthig*, and he composed two *Chiyi Khokbub (spyi'i khog 'bubs).* He said the commentary of *Sang Nying (gsang rnying)* should better be explained in the tradition of Rong Zom rather than in the tradition of Parkhab (spar khab).

Therefore, he composed the commentary on *Lama Jung* and the three texts above, in accordance with Rong Zom. He studied the complete *Madhyamika (tshig 'jug)* and others texts, such as *Phakor ('phag skhor*). From Shendor (gzhon rdor) he learned *Chienju (spyod 'jud), Labtue (bslab btus), Jowo'i Yidamkor (jo bo'i yi dam skor), Jordruk Chodruk (sbyor drug chos drug)* etc., and from Khenpo he studied *Khophuwa'i Kor (kho phu ba'i skor), Kharak Chokor (kha rag chos skor), Drubthap Gyatsho (sgrub thabs rgya mtsho), Chochung Gyatsha (chos chung brgya rtsa), Dulwalung ('dul ba lung)* and many more texts.

In addition to studying under those belonging to his own tradition, the Nyingma, he also was a student of Rang Jung Dorje (rang byung rdor rje, 1284-1339), the Karma Kagyudpa (bka' brgyud pa) hierarch. With him he studied *Jordruk Geksal (sbyor drug gegs sel), Naro Chodruk (na ro chos drug), Kusum Ngotrad (sku gsum ngo sprod), Gyalwa Gyamtsho (rgyal ba rgya mtsho), Chanrezi Gyalpo'i luk (spyan ras gzigs rgyal po lugs), Sangdus (gsang 'dus), Sambuti, Mahamaya, Shingje Shed Marnak (gshin rje gshed dmar nag)* etc., and with master Wang Tshul (dbang tshul) he studied *Jordruk (sbyor drug), Nyendrub (bsnyen sgrub), Lungkor (rlung skhor),* and many other texts. With about twenty other teachers, including the Sakyapa Lama Dampa Sonam Gyaltshan (sa skya pa lama dam pa bsad nams rgyal mtshan, 1312-1375), he studied *Semkey Chenpo (sems bsked chen mo)* and the nine profound teachings of Sakyapa, such as the *Lamdre (lam 'bras).* He wrote an article known as the *Shuyik Rinpoche Sergi Chodong (zhu yig rinpoche gser gyi mchod sdong)* based on the ground, path and result of the Sakyapa's nine *Lamdre;* he delivered it to Sakyapa Lama Dampa. In brief, he learned thoroughly almost all the arts of the different Traditions (except the dge lugs tradition, which

རྗེ་བཙུན་སྒྲོལ་མ།

originated after Longchen Rabjampa's time). He was always engaged in spiritual practice, from which he attained pure visions and received the blessing of Jampel Yang, Yangchenma, Miyowa, Phakmo, and Jetsun Drolma. The fame of his scholarship spread throughout the country. Thus he became all-pervading in discourse, debate and composition and became perfect in all arts and sciences. Like all Bodhisattvas, having submitted himself to the experience of listening and thought, he sought the wisdom of all-knowing. Having always been frustrated with the nature of world (Samsara) and having a strong aversion to this material world, he intended to fulfil his purpose by living only outside of towns and in the isolated place (nags khrod) which are always praised and recommended by the Buddhas and Bodhisattvas. At that time, like Sakyamuni Buddha, who saw the four causes (rkyen) which made him abandon the Royal Palace, he, the Longchenpa, had a similar experience. At the Institute (the Institute of Logic of Ngok Legpa'i Sherab), the monks of Khampa exhibited dishonesty and mischievousness; he felt frustrated and sad at this and decided to lead an ascetic life. At the time of his departure, the 'Lord Abbot' and the students requested him to forgive them and to continue to stay at the Institute. However, primarily because of the fortunes ofmasses, they could not prevent him from carrying on activities for the welfare of others. On the way, he met a monk near the funeral pyre (Dungten) of Venerable Ngok Lok Chenpo. He, too, requested him not to leave and showed his sadness. But after having heard about the details of the reasons for his departure, he also groaned about the Khampas' community. "Now, if you are really going, please write an article about the disgrace of the Khampas."[2] So, in a diverting style, he wrote a few lines on a piece of paper which they took and pasted on the Chair of the Congregation Hall. Unfortunately, although it was immediately seen by the Khampas, it was not noticed by anyone else. But his composition, like an appearance of cannibal demons in the town of Kalingga (ka ling yul du srin po rgyu ba bzhin...), based on thirty character of alphabet, gained much ground and became known all over Tibet and even in some neighbour countries. Thereafter he only engaged in meditational practices, wandering in uncertain places. Once, while he was staying as a Yogi of darkness (mun pa'i rnal 'byor; i.e., in complete dark place) for five months in the cave of Jama'i Chokla (rgya ma'i cogla), he heard the sweet sound of musical instruments and singing. He intended to find its source, but suddenly he met a sixteen year old girl, adorned in gold, turquoise and dressed in glossy silk clothes, riding on a well saddled horse; her face was covered by a web of golden cloth. Having caught the edge of her lower dress, he begged her to be considered her follower. She, took off her only crown and put it on the head of Kunkhen, saying, "From today onwards you will be blessed, protected and given the Siddhi (dngos grub) continuously."[3] Thereafter, he made a long retreat in contemplation (Samadhi) of *Desal Mitokpa (bde gsal mi rtog pa),* and made an array of omens to meet the Dharma of *Man Ngak Dzogpa Chenpo (man ngag rdzogs pa chen po).* One night a girl appeared before him and said, 'your Dharma-share (chos skal) is in Nyal. It is better now for you to go and get it back." When he woke up he was able to recollect his previous persona (bag chags) because of the dream, and he set out to Sho, where Legpa Gyaltshan was dwelling. He said, "You certainly have a doctrine which is important to me."[4] He requested Legpa Gyaltshan to give him the complete verbal authorisation in it. The Bodhisattva Legpa Gyaltshan asked, "Where have you come from, you Yogis, teacher and students?"[5] Tshul Thrim Dorje (tshul khrim rdo rje), the Longchenpa said, "We are from the centre (dbus) of Tibet. We are the Yogis of the Kingdom, and don't have permanent dwelling places. We came from Dangpo yesterday."[6] He again, asked, "You are sweet and intelligent. Where is your birth place? What is your name?"[7] In his testament (dying words), he said, "My previous Lama, Trulku Pema Ledreltshel, said that he would be born at the cave of Ü (dbus) in five years from his passing away. Maybe it is you, Yogi. Please show me your body."[8] He showed it by removing his clothes. It was exactly there, as he said in his previous testament. "Could you please recall your previous birth?" Tshul Dor (tshul rdor), the Longchenpa, said, "Listen Legpa Gyaltshan, yes, I do remember my previous birth. But have you comprehended the profound teachings which I taught you? Did you practice them accordingly? You have the empowerment and verbal authorisation of the *Heart drop of deity (khandro Nyingthig)* which I revealed as a treasure from Dagpo'i Danglung and also of the *Nyenpo Lhasum, Zaduki Judrup*, together with many instructions. "He proclaimed, "Give all those to me completely."[9]

Legpa Gyaltshan said, "O great Bodhisattva, it is wonderful that you have come back for the welfare of all beings and for us, your previous students. I, because of ignorance, could not recognise you as a Lama; please forgive me."[10] Having offered him a turquoise, a conch, fifty grams of gold (i.e. (equal five zho in Tibetan measurement) and seven scarves (pieces of cotton clothes), he said, "You are the Owner of Dharma, and it is not necessary to receive the verbal authorisation. I think it will suffice to present you with whatever is copied into Bupay (bu dpe) and the *Shokser (yellow paper) of Khandro Nyingthig.* "He (klong chenpa) said, "It is not like that, Legpa Gyaltshan, since birth has a beginning and an end. Thereby, the continuity of the authorisation of the Pitaka of advice is essential. So, perform the authorisation completely, as also empowered by me of the *Shokser (Yellow pages).*"[11] At that time, they put into writing whatever was there in the 'treasure text' of Thramo Drak (khra mo brag).

Thereafter, at twenty nine, as prophesied by his Yidam, he arrived at Samye and went toward the sacred place of Yartoe Cham (yar stod skyam), where a great mystic Kumaraja, (rig dzin ku ma radza, 1266-1343), who would become his chief teacher, was dwelling. On the way, he (long chen pa) met the chief of the Yakde (gyag sde), i.e., one who looked after Yak, who insisted him to go to the Karmapa's place, but he paid no attention to him and went on his own way. At the sacred place of upper Cham, he saw Kumaraja and the group of his disciples dwelling in the seventy tents. A night before Long Chenpa's arrival, Master Kumaraja had

རིག་འཛིན་ཀུ་མ་ར྄ཱ་ཛ།

dreamed that a wonderful heavenly bird had arrived. It was surrounded by many other birds. Later, they took all his books to the limits of all quarters. Having said, "There will be one who will hold my lineage,"[12] he felt very delighted. For instance, he (Long Chenpa) was not able to raise the doctrinal tribute; for that reason he felt a shooting pain in his mind. He thought, "Most probably it will be only I who has to leave the Guru because of being impeded by the doctrinal tribute." So, he thought, "It would be shameful to go in day time, but by tomorrow morning I should reach the lower terrace of the plateau." The Guru reflected on it with his prescient mind, and sent two monks to Long Chenpa saying that he should not be unpleasant about it. "We are going to offer the doctrinal tribute from the monastery itself." The Vidyadhara (rig dzin) Kumaraja told him, "Last night I dreamt that a wonderful heavenly bird had arrived, indicating your coming. You are the holder of the spiritual lineage of my doctrine, and the complete secret precept will be given to you." In order to increase the sadness of the group of disciples (so they could understand the sufferings of Samsara), the Vidyadhara (kumaraja) dwelled in no particular place or monastery. In that spring season especially, he changed residence nine times from one uninhabited valley to another; when they were almost settled, they had to move, so that he was left without proper food, and drink. Since Gangtsa village is a cold place, he became very weak and frustrated. In such a cold place, he was sustained only by three kilos of flour and twenty one pieces of quick-silver pills (dngul chu ril bu) for two months. When snow fell, he used to wrap himself in a piece of square cloth which he carried for wrapping up his provisions; during the day he used it for a mat. Likewise, he underwent lots of hardships and austerities for the sake of receiving instructions. That year, he received the empowerment, verbal authorisation and instruction of the mystic Nyingthig which he immediately put into the practice.

In the following year, he was given the Gongma empowerment and the Tantras, perceptions, secret instructions, and the guardian doctrine (bstan srung) of the *Dzogpa Chenpo Desum*,[13] like a fully filled vessel, and lama declared Long Chenpa as a successor to himself. Then, he promised him to do a retreat for six years.

At the age of thirty one, Kunkhen made a Mindrol (tshig gi smin, dbang gi grol) for many fortunate people in accordance with the teachings of Nyingthig at Nyiphu'i Shukseb (snyi phu'i shug gseb). At thirty-two, while making a retreat at Rimocan of Chimphu, he imparted the teaching of Nyingthig to the eight male (Yogis) and female (Yoginis) disciples, including the Yogi 'Odzer Gocha; during the blessing at the initiation of Troe Choe (spros bcas), Ngag Sungma, the Protectress, possessed one of the Yoginis and appeared in dancing. His disciples were unable to bear the splendour of the dakini. Then the Lama said, "This is a case of the assumption of Khandro; there is no consequence. I am the Yogi who has realised all objective appearances in one mind (snab sems ro gcig tu rtogs' pa'i rnal 'byor pa), so there won't be any hindrance from her."[14] At that time, the Yogini made a prostration to the Lama and, having looked at the mandala, she said, "Why is there no gathering of peacocks?" He said, "It is thought by the mind". She said, "In the doctrine of the gesture, how can it be possible by perception?"[15] Again having cast out the 'menji' of the vessel-support, she kept the three vessels in order. While they were doing the ritual performances in the proper and detailed manner, she having, folded the palms of her hands in devotion, said, "well-done!" When they removed the suffix 'Sa' from the letter 'Rigs', writing it as 'Rig', she said, "No, No, the word 'Rigs' is the correct word."[16] At the time of the recitation of the mantra, she asked them to say it after her, and she made both relevant and irrelevant sweet tones in the voice of a dakini. On the occasion of the main ritual offering (dngos gzhi) she sang a song as follows:

> *"It is rejoicing to separate mind from contemplation;*
> *How happy indeed is to part mind from meditation", ...*

Thus, she made a sweet religious metrical tune and said, "This offering is not perfect. So it is not proper to offer it". During the 'Tshok' sacrificial offering of obligation ceremony, especially, while offering the nectar to the Lama, she said, "Since it is an object of religious utility (dam rdzas) of the Dakinis, you must attend to it."[17] So she offered it to him completely. At that time, even the assembly of disciples experienced the thought of understanding of wisdom spring up in their minds. They sang a song and danced. Then they developed a single-minded realisation which was beyond the usual sleep, having seen the true forms of Demi-Gods, Dakinis, Dharma protectors and many others. One of the dark girls said that an offering of flour was missing. Having transformed into a white daka, the Damcanpa (a tantric deity) said, " A piece of raw meat (dmar rgyan) is missing from among my sacrificial objects (gtor ma)."[18] Jowo Danglha (jobo mdang lha), the protector, having come in the form of a white daka riding on a white horse, tried to persuade the saint to give a sacrificial object (gtor ma), while giving him a sacrificial object (dmar gtor); he declined. Then the Lama was honoured with the ritual umbrella by the Dakinis. While making a circumambulations, they recited loudly the syllables Hum ( ) and Phat ( ) and others.[19] and there arouse a great noise and many other miracles. Then one of the Yogis said,

"Today the earth and sky are revolting and may be it will cause our bodies fall into pieces."[20] Having thought that, he felt terribly frightened. Likewise, the protectors 'Odde Gunggyal (od de gung rgyal), Nanchen Thanglha (gnan chen thang lha), and seven brothers and sisters of Menmo, came to receive their Terma (gterma).

རྡོ་རྗེ་ཕག་མོ།

At that time Dorje Phakmo (rdo rje phag mo),[21] of a sky- blue complexion, being adorned with Ornaments and bones, appeared truly. One of the disciples asked, "What do you want"? She said, "Tonight being a wild time, I have come to observe the worthy students. By the way, how is the Lama? Is he in good health?"[22] He (the disciple) again asked her, "This year being a year of much diseases and misfortune, how will he be?" The Dakini said: "As he is a manifestation of Lord Buddha, how do you students dare to think of becoming a hindrance to him. You see! He is just a reflection for beings to be converted."[23] Then she asked Lama Longchenpa, "Don't you know about the arrival of Vimalamitra in Tibet?" Longchenpa asked, "How long will he be staying there?"[24] She said, "Most probably he will stay till the end of the Year of the Sheep, although, there is no certainty of his staying in Tibet. It depends on the beings to be converted (bdul bya)." "Well then, I am admonished by

Lama Kumaraja to behave like this." "Oh, yes, you are right. I am the one who induced him to act like that. If I contemplate alone, will I be able to realise the 'Odlus' (Luminous body)? or would there be any benefit to sentient beings if I work for the welfare of others? How long may I live?" he asked. "Even if you achieved the luminous body, you must benefit sentient beings. Their welfare will be very much advanced. Including this year, you will live thirty years more."[25] He asked, "Who are my Dharma protectors?" She answered, "Many, many, almost all the protectors of your Lama (Kumaraja). Especially, you have Dorje Yudronma (rdo rje gyu sgron ma) as your Dharma protector, Likewise, your intention to do welfare is towards the direction of the south-west. In your next life, you will be more successful than this life in doing welfare to others." "Well, was this the preaching explained from the Khandro Nyingthig? Is it a suitable for me to confer instructions and empowerment," he asked. "Oh! yes, you are right. Since you are the Master of Dharma, there is indeed no problem in teaching it,"[26] she said. Once again he asked, "Is the public not going to hold deceitful views of me?" "What truth is there to the speech of people? The fortunate people will willingly come together. And what can one say about unfortunate people? It is said that they used to abuse Lord Buddha too,"[27] she said. "So, should I propagate the Dharma of Nyingthig in the locality of Dorje?" he asked. "You should do it there, since that is the place where all the Dakinis gather naturally."[28] He was also told clearly about the prophecy of the treasures of Bumthang in Bhutan. He asked, "Will I be able to meet the Great Guru (Padmasambhava)?" She said, "On the upper part of the three hill at the right side of the small Drakchung Newa (brag chung ne ba) facing towards the west. There you will meet the Guru Padma". He asked, "When will I meet Vimala? She said, "You are Vimala."[29] "Will this realisation of my perception achieve the ultimate reflection of the Nyingthig," he asked. "There is nothing wrong at all in achieving the extreme limit of realisation,"[30] she said.

Lopen Rindor (slob dpon rin rdor) asked, "Where is Pang Gangwa Rinchen Dorje (i.e., las 'brel tshal) dwelling?" She, having pointed her finger at the Lama (Longchenpa), said, "He is here with us."[31] In this connection, Longchenpa said, "I am supposed to take my next birth in Bumthang. How can I do that?" She said, "One does not always take birth as planned."[32] You have to wander in the realm of Samboghakaya because you, as (Pema Ledreltshal), after revealing the treasure, could have practised in a hidden manner. If you had done like that, you might have achieved the Celestial Samboghakaya for your own sake at that time and in that way there might have been much benefit to others. Since you were not able to practice in the hidden way, you passed away at such a young age. Now, when you are reborn, taking the path of the celestial vision is like being in the realm of Samboghakaya for a little while." "When shall I achieve the Lhagmed body (the entireness of body)?" he asked. "If you meditate alone, you may achieve it within this life. But, doing welfare to others, you will indeed realise it in the Bardo stage. Having reincarnated in Bumthang, you will do welfare to others. After that, you will reach the western paradise of Ugyen Rinpoche, where you will assume the manner of Enlightenment (Buddhahood)," she said. "Which of these two Nyingthig is going to benefit sentient beings? Is it the Vima Nyingthig or Khandro Nyingthig?" he asked. "Both are beneficial. But the Vima Nyingthig will last only for a hundred years and Khandro Nyingthig will last for five hundred years, starting from right now,"[33] she replied. Then the Lama, having expanded his understanding, arose from his seat and sang a song of Vajra:-

Happy indeed are this and future lives;
Cheerful indeed is the Intermediate stage,
by means of knowing Oneself;
Now, here comes one happy life after another;
I offer this devotional song to the Triple Gems;
May the assembly of Dakinis be happy.

Again, having seen numerous vision of Dakinis, finally they all dissolved into the Lama. Then the Lama was seen sometimes in the form of Samboghakaya. Once, on the 28th day, from the south-west came the great Guru. He was dressed in a glossy silk cloth and 'Za 'od gi ber Sha ba'i mnyen zhu can, and he was surrounded by a great retinue; they were seen to melt into the Lama. On that night, a Dakini, adorned with bones, was praying while walking around in the sky. Then three dark maroon girls danced, uttering the following words:-

"We have come from the place Sukhavati;
To observe the worthy students;
To observe the purity of vows and precepts;
Do the welfare to the others, you, a noble son".

At the time of the mystical religious service of inner offering (Nang mchod), to the right of the great Guru was seated Vimala and to the left Dorje Phakmo. In front were many Dakinis blowing trumpets (made of the human thigh-bone, used in temples). Behind, many mantrikas (snangpa) were dancing. The Lama stood up in the centre of the

Dakinis, who were circumambulating and singing, and he said,

> *"Oh, Yogis, it is a moment of happiness and peace;*
> *To night is the time of Akanista heaven;*
> *In the palaces of peace and of wrath of our body,*
> *Will expand the victorious mandala of our emptiness;*
> *The Buddha is not outside but within Oneself..., and*
> *The meditator who remains in one-pointed mind,*
> *Will see whatever is pleasant without holding obstruction.*
> *The continuation and existence of mind is empty.*
> *Whatever comes to mind is the manifestation of wisdom."*

རྡོ་རྗེ་གཡུ་སྒྲོན་མ།

That time, the Dorje Yudronma, having arrived together with Karmo Chedun (dkar mo mched bdun), requested him to visit her locality. The Lama said, "Should I stay in your place all the time?" "It would be a great pleasure if you would stay always, but you had better stay only till the first part of the winter," she said. Kunkhen Longchenpa asked, " For what purpose do you want me to stay?" "I am the follower of the Guru's Solemn Vows. So I am after the treasure," said she. Then he said, "What are you doing here? That kind of Dharma is yonder. The practitioner has passed away". "Although the Dharma is there, its meaning is here,"[34] she said. Having prophesied about the Dharma protectors, she said: "Since it is a wild time , hindrance may be coming to your life. So it will be better for you to propagate only a few instructions". He asked, "Who will bring my treasure papers?" "Silence, silence, it is indeed our work,"[35] she said. "Do you remember the blessing of the Siddhi which I gave at dbu ru?" she said. Having remembered the one in the cave of Cogla, he said, "She was Dorje Yudronma." "No, no, she was Dorje Phakmo, Didn't you recognise her?"[36] she said. Thus are the deeds performed by worldly beings (rdo rje gyu sgron ma) and they are part of the excellent Siddhi given by the "Das pa'i gzugs (rdo rje phag mo).

Then he, having focused chiefly on a teaching of the Virile Semen (thig le),[37] asked, "How are the three empowerments given to the Dakini (rten can)?" "The empowerment is necessary for those practitioners having a consort," She said; "for fully ordained monks it is not necessary; for them only a thought of the yid-rig will suffice."[38] At the moment of identification (ngo sprod) in the meditational, he asked, "Which one is correct, to keep comprehension (rtog-pa) in an unoriginated state or to keep the mind in an unthinking state (rtsis med)?" "What adverse effect can there be for comprehension? Identify with the great immensity (space) of the deliverance from being, Yedrol Longyang Chenpor Ngotroe Chi (ye grol klong yangs chen po ngo sprod cig),"[39] the Dakini answered.

"Well, why is it necessary for me to expound the Nyingthig, when there are so many Preceptors (lung byed pa) like Karmapa, Rinchen Lingpa?" he said. "I am not satisfied with the way they have preached. Such preachers can be found in forest and cave, but it is not appropriate to receive this particular instruction from them. It is indeed necessary to have its master," she said. When she was asked about the treasure of the Rinchen Lingpa, she said, "To be frank, I have no idea." He asked, "What is the cause of my realisation without my contemplation?"[40]

Do I possess divine power to be contemplated?
Do I possess any mantras to be recited?
Do I have any place to be offered?

"Don't you know that I am always there with all the Yogis who possess the solemn Vows and infallible knowledge. There is no separation from you in my all births,"[41] she said,

Then, "what about the wealth of Lhacam at Chimphu?" he asked. It is on a flat rock like an offering of eatables substances presented to a deity. "It is still not the right time to discover it," she said. "When will the treasure of Vimala be discover?" he asked. "After fifteen years, a white mantrika (ascetic) will take out the teaching and propagate it.[42] The four profound volumes will come into your hands,"[43] she said.

Then in the 11th of the month, Longchenpa sent a Yogi 'Odzer Gocha, to bring the book. While he was bringing the book, it was penetrated and surrounded by a rainbow. Particularly, on the night of the arrival of the holy text at Chukpo Drak (phyug po brag) near the Chatiya (Stupa) which lies at the bottom end of Zungkhar valley, the shining of the rainbow was seen even from Rimochen by all the yogis and yoginis.

After performing all the necessary sacrificial offerings, he opened the Dharma door of the sacred instructions of the Khandro Nyingthig. At that very moment many wonderful events occurred. On that evening, from the illumination of the brightness of the night, the reflection of the Dharmakaya whirling in the celestial sphere, which is pure from the beginningless time, could be seen; from the brilliance of its illumination appeared the mode of the Samboghakaya. And because of the outer brightness, the body of Nirmanakaya expanded, and he saw the manner of the appearance of the six realms. The great sound of the Dharma and the great essence of existence could not be calculated, even by the great astrologer (tis po che). And he bestowed the blessing of the great essence on the assembled Lamas, Yidam and Dakinis. The Dakini made the ritual of identification (ngo sprod) visible.

Then, at the time of the recording of the sacred instruction of the KhandroYangthig, the Great Guru Padma in the meditational form of the Thuk Drub (thugs sgrub). On the right Yeshe Tshogyal, and on the left Yudronma. One of the Yoginis who possessed the complete marks of a Dakini had seen them checking the text. Yeshe Tshogyal, in particular, having appeared in human form for a period of six days, gave Longchenpa a clear explanation of 'example, meaning, gesture' of the Khandro Nyingthig. After having received the blessing of all the instructions together with entrustment, he then had a wonderful imagination and a power of identification and of preaching, which he never had before. The many letters which had not been clear to him he now understood naturally. Even in those days the Longchenpa, the second Samantabhadra Buddha, who turned the Wheel of Dharma of the *Gongter Jatsho'i Dorje (dgong gter rgya mtsho'i rdo rje),* was considered the most profound and supreme among all Nyingthig instructors in Tibet and Bhutan. So, it is worthy to esteem this system of doctrine.

The other teachings which did not adhere to this teaching are to be known as the butter lamp of the diagram and are also worthy of respect.

Likewise, most of the teachings took place there at Chimphu, although in the index it is written Gangri Thodkar, since the work of arrangement took place there.

རེ་མ་ཏི།

Again, this Dharma became like the heart blood of the Dakini. Even in this place, Chimphu, being a holy place for the assembly of the Dakinis, three roots (rtsa ba) expanded limitlessly.[44] The holding of a peacock umbrella above the head of the Lama was seen. And while drawing the line of the mandala (using a rope), the Red Girl held the other end of the rope. While setting out the 'Rek sha' (Figure), a lady Ser Yu'i Lentsher (gser gyu'i len tsher) made an enquiry about it.. At the time of the 'Gongma' empowerment, there gathered seven disciples. Suddenly blood came out from their noses. Then Lama Longchenpa said, "It is all because of an excess of numbers. In this empowerment only three are eligible to take part. So, you four leave."[45] At that moment a rainbow emerged in the Empowerment Hall. Then the Namdru Remati (nam gru re ma ti) appeared in reality and said "Why didn't you give me the "Torma" (sacrificial object)? I have done much difficult work for a long time."[46] Having explained clearly about herself, the Chief, and her retinues, she demonstrated great miracles and prophesied about the treasure. The Longchenpa said :

> *I, who have opened the treasure of inner most illumination (understanding),*
> *It is not necessary for me to have the Chasm treasure;*
> *I am satisfied whether I possess the treasure or not;*
> *I don't distinguish between the fortunate and unfortunate;*
> *I am the Yogi, who has realised pristine nature;*
> *Don't boast to me about yourself as a Protector of the treasure.*

On the occasion of the introduction of the *Jabchoe (rgyab chos)* and *Rinpoche Sangwa* of the *Khandro Yangthig*, many people saw her (yeshe Tshogyal) consecrating by holding the vessel. They suddenly stood up and prostrated to her with deep respect and devotion. During the introduction of the intermediate stage 'bardo'[47] and dream stage 'Odsal Bubjuk' (od gsal sbubs 'jug), the Dakinis became delighted, "To this Dharma of mine (yashi) the non-human are showing a better supplication and prayer than the Human beings; you should keep this in mind,"[48] he said.

While performing the introduction of the 'Odsal Yeshe', the entire cosmic space was filled by Dakinis with folded hands (folding the palms of their hands in devotion). At night, a female protector of the mantras descended and performed dances. Then Longchenpa said to her, "I used to make visible the Nyingthig instructions in this way. Are you (the dharma protectors and Dakinis) feeling happy?" he asked. "Even Guru Rinpoche and his consort, Yeshe Tshogyal used to instruct in this way. Otherwise, there is no way to know like this." "It is wonderful, really wonderful,"[49] she said.

All the Dakinis were delighted. "Furthermore, the Yudronma, who is praying from Ugyen Dzong, is very much delighted," she said. Then appeared a Great Damcan (mystic protector) and insisted that he, Longchenpa, go to Ugyen Dzong, i.e., to Gangri Thodkar. Again, the Yudronma proclaimed, "You will have thirty disciples who will be able to perform welfare. Among them seven disciples will be a great benefit to sentient beings. And nine of them will be specially good. So, having been able to meet this Guru (Longchenpa), you are the most fortunate ones."[50]

On the occasion of the Entrustment of the Guardian of Buddhism, the female butcher named Song Drubma (srong sgrub ma), a protector deity, appeared and requested Longchenpa not to recite her Sadhana (sgrub thabs).

Likewise, in the evening at the end of the entire instructions and empowerments of the Khandro Nyingthig, the lama said, "Last night, the Siddhi (dngos grub) was bestowed by Dakinis. And nobody is going to come tonight. So, put water in an earthen winepot." While filtering whatever was there, it could fill only a small cup. The lama said, "It is not enough; put in a little more water and filter it." Doing so, he had more than enough wine to make almost all the assemble drunk. "This is what we called the miraculous transformation of substance,"[51] he said. After that, Yudronma insisted that he (the Lama) visit her locality at Gangri Thodkar. The Lama gave a gesture of acceptance by nodding his head. She, feeling very happy left before him to prepare the place. Soon after that Namdo appeared and requested the Lama not to go there. "See! Even though I (Longchenpa) explained the Dharma like this, you, non-human, have not understood it. It is the miraculous character of mind to be happy or unhappy. It would be well if you come to wherever I am living."[52] It is said that while making the initiation of Samadhi (meditation), she recalled what she was supposed to do. "Where were you yesterday," he asked. "I was at Drok [brog] (an uncultivated land)," she said. At that time many cattle disease spread widely and many cattle fell victim. Thereafter, all the Yogis and Yoginis made the mandala offering with their clothes and jewels. And while they made a solemn vow to practice teaching, Longchenpa said: "For this Dharma of mine, there will be many generous people and there will be many people who will strive to keep their promises and to put the Sadhana into practices." Again, having said the teaching to the 'Odsal Bubjuk (dream stage), he reminded them, "Such sacred instructions are very rare in the world. If a 'snod',[53] is performed, he may accomplish the illumination body soon."[54]

Then he departed from Samye Chimphu. At Chukpo Drak he made a sacrificial offerings. There he was given a warm reception by Yudronma. Then, at the time of his invitation to Shukseb near Gangri Thodkar, a Dakini having entered into one of the Yogis, requested the Lama to go to Ugyan Dzong. There, at the artificial grove of Gangri Thodkar ugyen Dzong 'Odzer Tin, he set *Khandro Yangthig* into writing at the request of Yogi 'Odzer Gocha. At that time, the sky was filled with a rainbow and there appeared exhaustless miracles and visions of Dakinis, which everyone witnessed.

In the meantime, Longchenpa went to his Guru (kumaraja) to clarify the critical explanation of the instruction (religious precept). He delighted his Guru by establishing a meditation centre wherever he stayed. Having realised the ultimate tranquillity of this phenomenon, he didn't take the opportunity to become the head of any monastery. He honoured his Lama five times with all his possessions.

On 8th, 10th and 25th of each month, he observed as a day of the worship, and made grand sacrificial offerings to please those Dakas and Dakinis.[55] At Gangri Thodkar, taking the secret path of 'Odsal Thodgyal ('od gsal thod rgal) he, having gone to the place of the Rikpa Tshey Pheb (rig pa tshad phebs), meditated in the womb of the Yogi form. He was blessed by the Yidam many times. Acharya Vimala, particularly, had shown his face and told him (Longchenpa) to write a summary, of precise meaning and easy to comprehend, of his 'Vima Nyingthig'. He indicated Zhen Nu'i Sangay (gzhan nu'i sangs rgyas), one of the present disciples, as an incarnation of Kumaraja. Apart from this, he also prophesied that there will come forth seven disciples of Zhen Nu'i Mingchan (gzhan nu'i ming can; zhen nu as a name) marked by a letter Ah on their noses, who will hold and propagate this Dharma (lama yangthig). The Lama Yangthig, the gem ornament, was classified into thirty five treatises.

In the Female Earth Hare Year, he had also shown his manifested face to Vidyadhara Jigme Lingpa three times at a large cemetery in the forest of Chimphu. Having prayed constantly, he received the complete blessing as if between man and man. Then he, Longchenpa, handed over to him ('jigs med gling pa) a volume of the book (glegs bam), saying that all the meaning of the concealed sacred instructions, such as the *Shingta Chenmo (shing rta chen mo),* and others, will be clarified by this text. Having commanded all the teachings which proceeded after the sacred instruction and benediction, the remembrance of a religious disposition is very clear like unpolluted sky. Then arose a partial understanding in all the sacred instructions and the Philosophy system of Chotshul

Gyatsho (chos tshul rgya mtsho) and Kunkhen Lama. Because of this auspicious sign, the problem of the doctrines, which were difficult to collect, was solved permanently. The printing press at Degay Tsadpo (sde dge btsad po) and later on at Kongpo, Yoru and Rinmin Chimphu reproduced the gem ornament *Yangthig,* the text of Kunkhen, which spread widely throughout Tibet. Especially the people who encountered it looked with great respect and devotion on it as a work and power of the second Buddha. Likewsie, Vimala, having pointed his right finger in the direction of the Yuru Zha (dbu ru zha) monastery, prophesied the necessity to renovate it.

དམ་ཅན་རྡོ་རྗེ་ལེགས་པ།

Longchenpa went to Yuru Zha Monastery. while it was under renovation, many skulls which were under it, leapt up into the sky. Then, just by pointing his finger in the mode of the profound meditation, he was able to drawn them under the ground. And from behind the pinnacle (dbu rtse) of a monastery he took out gold to increase the fund for renovation. Damcan Dorje Legpa (a tantrik deity), having become a boy, assisted a carpenter daily. Since they were unable to bring down two big stones by any means or force, he offered sacrificial objects (gtor ma) to the Dharma protector by way of ordering him [to help]. With great assertion, he placed a dharma text and a Buddha Statue together on the stones. Thereafter, they were able to remove the rock without much effort or pain. Having restored the destroyed texts about the suppression of *dam sri*, which were in the various skulls, he once again replaced them under thevery same place. There was a heavy storm; because of the rain of earth and stone, people ran away. The skulls having leapt up, collided with each another. One of the biggest skulls, which expanded into the sky, was brought under control by the miracles of *Dam sri*,[56] by means of a 'glance' and by the meditation of Drakshul Rabtu Barwa (drag shul rab tu 'bar ba).[57] As a sign of powerful meditation, he was looked upon as the true form of Guru Drakpo. Again, the skulls were buried under the foot of the Stupa Thramen (phra men).

At the time of consecration, many wonderful forms of bodies were shown. The Buddha, the Maitreya (the Buddha of the future) and the sixteen famous sthaviras Neyten Chudruk (gnas brten bcu drug) had shown their smiling faces everywhere. Jampa, having raised his finger, gave a prophecy that at the end of his birth he would become a perfect Buddha as a Tathagata of the Rirab Margyal Tshan (ri rab mar rgyal mtshan in the sphere of Pedam Tsekpa (pedma brtseg pa).

Then he gave an instruction of the unexcelled doctrine of mysticism, *Sangwa Lana Medpa (gsang ba bla na med pa),* to a gathering on both shores of the Kyichu river at upper U. He made a large sacrificial offering, arranged in a circle. He also often made a good donation to a school for religious instruction at Sangphu.

He saw a fearful face straight from the hill of Kongpo (the country of ravines of a province of Tibet lying to the south-east of Lhasa and the East of Tsethang). So, having apprehended the coming of a dispute in the territory of Tibet, he departed for Bumthang (Centre Bhutan).

ཐར་པ་གླིང་།

At that time, Bumthang was a district where the teachings of Buddha were practised by only a few people. Therefore, people were quite wild and found it difficult to bring themselves into the main stream of the Buddhas' path of liberation. By and large, he was successful in setting up a monk community with a large number of monks, which was named Tharpaling monastery. He appointed Lopen Sangay Kunga (slop dpon sangs rgya kun dga) to be an in charge of the Community. Then he propagated the teachings of the Dzogchen (Great Fulfilment) and the common teachings of the early textual translations.

The disciples and followers who came under the power of the Bodhisattva Drimed 'Odzer were mostly from the following places:

Yerpa Latey (yer pa la stod), Zablung (zab lung),
Kongpo (rkong po), Tsari, Lhodrak, Paro (spa gro),
Memlok, Ngalong (rnga long), Bumthang,
Shar Lahok (shar la 'og),etc.

The most significant of his contributions to Bhutan during his stay was the construction of eight large Monasteries (gling brgyad). They are :

མོན་ལོག་ཀུན་བཟང་གླིང་།

1. Babron Tharpaling (bab ron thar pa gling).
2. Shingkhar Dechenling (shing mkhar bde chen gling).
3. Tang Ugyencholing (stangs au rgyan cho gling).
4. Kurteo Kunzangling (ku re stod kun bzangs gling).
5. Nyenlung Dre Changling (rnan lung 'bras bcang gling).
6. Khotang Pedmaling (kho thang pedma gling).
7. Menlok Kunzangling (man log kun bzang gling).
8. Paro Samtenling (spra gro bsam gtan gling).

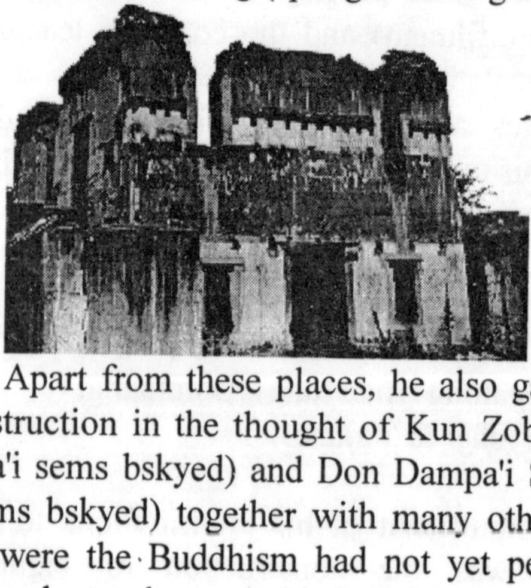

བསམ་གཏན་གླིང་།

Apart from these places, he also gave empowerment and instruction in the thought of Kun Zobpa'i Semkay (kun rzob pa'i sems bskyed) and Don Dampa'i Semkay (don dam pa'i sems bskyed) together with many other instructions, in places were the Buddhism had not yet penetrated. He was able, thereby to place suitable individuals on the path to

Nirvana, by the light of the Dharma. During his stay in Bhutan, he lived mainly in Bumthang Tharpaling Monastery and hid many sacred teachings, like the *Kun Zang Gongdue (kun bzang dgongs 'dus),* etc., in the Chamber of Tharpaling, before his departure for Lhasa

Immediately after his arrival in Lhasa, he payed a visit to Lord Buddha at Jokhang Temple. There he was blessed by means of a ray of the light which came forth from the centre of the forehead. Because of this wonderful event, he was able to recollect his previous birth as Panditas in Khotan and Rajgir (Near Nalanda, India). At Lhasa, the monks gave him a clerical procession of welcome. In between Lhasa and Ramache, he gave a grand sermon like the Semkay Chenmo (sems bskyed chen mo), and others, sitting on the valuable seat prepared for delivering religious discourses. He also, subdued many arrogant people by means of knowledge and injunction, people who tried to challenge his spiritual progress by personal attempts or through other means. So, he having made them perfect in their perception, the knowledge of reality grew in their minds. Because of that he became known by the name Kunkhen Choeje (Lord of Dharma, Omniscience). Once again, while paying a visit to Lord Buddha at Jokhang Temple, a ray of light proceeded from the body of the Buddha, like purified gold, and gradually, emerging from the surface of his head, he saw a succession of Seven Buddhas Sangay Rabdhun (Sangs rgyas rab bdun) who preceded Gautama Buddha: Kasyapa ('od srung), Kanaka muni, (gser thub),and others; The Buddha presiding over the healing art (smon bla); The Degay (bde dgyes); The Avaloketesvara the King of sky; The Gyalwa Jatsho (rgyal ba rgya mtsho), and group of the protectors of Buddhism. Apart from this, he, very often saw Great Guru (Padmasambhava), Guru Drakpo, Dampa Rigja (dampa rigs brgya), Drup Chen

Kagyad (sgrub chen bka' brgyad) and others, and also many Buddhas and Bodhisattvas, who later insisted that he compose a religious text and received full verbal authorisation. Longchenpa entered his mind into the profundity of Kuntu Zangpo (Samantabadhra), becoming omniscient and unchangeable. The wisdom received after this was mingled together with the blessing of the Buddhas. His composite self was inseparable from that of word of the Buddha. His commentaries were mainly composed to bestow an immense relief from suffering in order to rest in complete happiness (Nirvana), especially for those beings whose minds are untamed like an elephant's and who are loaded down with all kind of suffering, who are ignorantly starting on their journey toward the ocean of the Samsara (cyclic existence).

His commentaries were divided into three sections of knowledge: (a) The outer (General) section; (b) The inner (Esoteric science) section; (c) The Science of Metaphysics (Sunyata) section.

(a) The outer (General) section:

(i) Texts on Grammar and vocabulary:

1. yi ge'i sdeb sbyor la 'jug pa rin chen sne ma che chung gnyis.
2. rig pa klog pa'i don bsdus.
3. sgra bzhi'i mtshams sbyor.
4. klog gi bstan bcos zla ba gsal byed.
5. sdeb sbyor la 'jug pa ni ma'i shing rta.
6. lci yang gi gnas pa rin po che'i sde mig.
7. mnon brdzod la 'jug pa me tog gi 'khri shing.
8. snan nag gi bstan bcos me tog rgyas pa'i skyed mos tshal.

9. dper brdzod kyi gnas nes pa klu shing me tag.
10. spel ma'i gnas la 'jug pa tshangs pa'i gsung dbyang te.

(ii) Works illustrating the principles of poetics, didactic stories, verses, poetical texts in praise of various Boddhisattvas:

11. mi 'm ci kun tu dgah ba'i zlos gar.
12. gzhan nu zhi ba'i rtogs pa brdzod pa me tog gi chun po.
13. blo gsal ri bong go rtogs brdzod.
14. legs par gdams pa lha'i rna bo che lta bu'i gtam.
15. po ta la kun tu dga' ba'i gtam.
16 legs par sbyar ba'i snan nag sla ba'i 'khri shing rab tu bzang po.
17. me tag gi ra ba
18. nags kyi gtam padma dkar po.
19. nags kyi gtam gangs ri'i rgyan.
20. nags kyi gtam kun tu bzang po.
21. nags kyi gtam ku mu da'i 'khri shing.
22. nags tshal kun tu dga' ba'i gtam.
23. chos kyi sdom bzhi dri ma med pa'i gtam.
24. chos bzhi rin po che'i phreng ba.
25. slo dpon brtags pa'i rab tu 'byed pa.
26. rab byung brtag pa'i rab tu 'byed pa.
27. skye bo brtags pa'i rab tu byed pa.
28. mkhas blun brtag pa'i rab tu byed pa.
29. bshes gnen brtag pa'i rab tu byed pa.
30. chos dang chos min brtag pa'i rab tu byed pa.
31. shin tu bya dka' ba'i gnas kyi dper brdzod yi ger bkod pa.
32. dbyangs nes pa can gyi rgyan.
33. dus la mnon par skyo ba'i rabs.

34. rang la gros su btab pa'i rabs.
35. thar pa la bskul ba'i rabs.
36. bde bar gshegs pa'i thugs rdze la bskul ba'i rabs.
37. phyogs kyi sde snad 'dzon pa rnam la gtam du bya ba'i rabs.
38. bla ma dam pa la zhu ba zhu yid rin chen gser gyi mchod sdong.
39. zhu yig padma stong ldan.
40. zhu yig nor bu'i dra ba.
41. zhu yid rma bya'i na mo
42. phyogs kyi slo ma la bsnags pa lha'i rna sgra.
43. sbyin bdag la bsnags pa rin po che'i bang mdzod.
44. dri ba ni shu pa'i lan rgya cher bshad pa.
45. sems dang ye she kyi dri ba'i lan rgya cher bshad pa.
46. mkha' grub dam pa rnam kyi myang 'das che chung.
47. bstan pa snigs pa'i skyo ba bsam pa.
48. rgyu la khams 'dus pa me tog phreng ldan.
49. rkkyen la khams 'dus pa ka kha sum cu.
50. gnis ka la khams 'dus pa dran pa'i me long.
51. skye bo dga' skyed pa glu-gar gyi rtsed mo.
52. byis pa bzhad gar slong pa spre hu'i zlos gar.
53. 'jigs rten lugs la 'jug pa mdzang kyi 'phrul yig.
54. bde bar gshegs pa la bstod pa rna bo che'i byangs snan.
55. yum la stad pa yid bzhin nor bu.
56. yon tan tshad med par bstad pa.
57. bsam gyis mi khyab par bstod pa.
58. dpe las 'das par bstod pa.
59. spyan ras gzigs la bstod pa lha'i sil snan.
60. rta mgrin la bstod pa glog gi phreng ba.
61. 'jam dpal dkar po la bstod pa mu tig gi phreng ba.

62. dmar po la bstad pa mi 'am ci'i dbyangs snan.
63. ser po la bstod pa dri za'i rgyud mangs.
64. snon po la stod pa sprin gyi na ro.
65. 'phags ma dbyangs can ma la bstod pa gzhon nu mchog dga'i dbyangs ku mu ta'i phreng ba padma'i dra ba.
66. 'phags ma nor rgyun ma la bstod pa gser gyi sprin phung.
67. ku ru kulle la bstod pa dbang po'i rgyud mangs.
68. dug sel ma la bstod pa klu'i gtsug rgyan.
69. 'od zer can ma la bstod pa 'jigs pa kun sel.
70. dpal mo la bstod pa dbang po'i me tog.
71. phag mo dkar mo la bstod pa dpal gyi phreng 'dzin.
72. dmar mo la bstod pa dus kyi phreng ba.
73. nag mo la bstod pa dnos grub kun byung.
74. mi gyo dkar po la bstod pa malli ka'i phreng ba.
75. dmar po la bstod pa dus mtShams kyi sprin.
76. snon po la bstod pa 'byung po kun 'dul.
77. sgrol ma la bstod pa dpyid kyi na ro.
78. tshogs bdad la bstod pa nor bu'i mdzod.
79. dbang phyug la bstod pa lha'i me tag.
80. khyab 'jug la bstod pa klu'i na ro.
81. dbu ma la bstod pa ku mu ta'i gnen.
82. tshangs pa la bstod pa rgya mtsho'i rba rlags.
83. dus kyi lha la bstad pa dpyid kyi thig le.
84. ri dang rgya mtsho la bstod pa phyogs kyi na ro.
85. mchims phu'i gnas la bstod pa dus bzhi'i me tag.
86. yer pa'i gnas la bstod pa padma'i phreng ba.
87. gangs ri thod dkar gyi gnas la bstad pa rol mo'i dbyang snan.
88. lum pa'u gtsugs lag la bstod pa rgya mtsho'i rba rlabs.

89. bsam yas kyi yul gyi bkod pa gsal bar byed pa gangs ri'i rgyan.
90. gsang phu'i chos grawa la bsnags pa yon ton phreng tshogs.
91. zhawa padma dbang chen gyi gtsug lag khang la bstod pa rol mo'i sprin phung.
92. dkar chag rgyas par rcis kyi yi ge zhib mo.
93. bsdus pa no mtshar dran byed.

(b) The inner (Esoteric science) section, consists of two sub-sections.

(i) First commentary, which pertains to the Doctrine of Essential Causal Characteristics (mtshan nid rg'u yi theg pa) :

94. byams pa'i chos lna'i spyi'i don 'grel dus lam gyi rnam par bzhag pa rin chen them skas rtsa 'grel dang bcas pa.
95. mnon rtogs rgyan gyi lus rnam bzhag gi gsal byed rgyan gyi snang ba.
96. 'dul ba ka ri ka'i gsal byed 'od kyi sne ma.
97. rang rgyud shar gsum gyi don bsdus de kho na nid la 'jug pa.
98. dbu ma thal 'gur gyi gnas gsal ba rab tu mi gnas pa'i don bsdus.
99. bde ba gnis rab tu bya ba la 'jug pa.
100. de'i man nag lam rim gsal ba.
101. sems spyog don gyi snying po.
102. lung sbyor rin po chec'i phreng ba.
103. sems bskyed rin po che gser gyi me tog.
104. bslo bya rgyal sras lam bzang.

105. zab mo. mdo lna'i don bshad.
106. smon lam rgya mtsho'i snying po.
107. gcod yul dag pa'i lam khyer.
108. phung po gsum pa'i nams len.
109. 'da' dka' ye shes kyi sgom thabs la sogs paho.

(ii) Second commentary, which pertaines to the Doctrine of mystical results :

110. bshad pa'i gnas gsal bar bstan pa yid bzhin rin po che'i mdzod rtsa ba.
111. 'grel pa padma dkar po dang bcas pa. sgyu 'phrul dra ba chen po'i chos kyi rnam grang las :-
112. gsang ba'i snying po de kho na nid nes pa'i spyi don yid kyi mun sel-gsang 'grel phyogs bcu mun sel yin nam.
113. bsbus don ma rig mun sel.
114. rigs lna ye she snang ba rnams dang.
115. chos spyod thams cad kyi mnon par rtogs pa'i rgyud kyi mnon par rtogs pa'i rgyud kyi bshad 'grel byang chub ljon shing.
116. rgyud sde bzhi'i spyi don bshad pa rdo rje 'byung ba.
117. dam tshig gsum bkod kyi rnam bshad ni ma'i 'od zer.
118. phrin sgrub cho ga'i skor la. sgu 'phrul zhi khro'i skongs bshags kyi cho ga rgyas pa.
119. de'i le'u lag bsdus pa.
120. bla ma'i phrin sgrub rin po che'i sgron me.
121. thugs rje chen po 'khor ba dong sprung gi cho ga padma cod pan.

122. kun rigs rtsa ba'i dkyil 'khor du slob ma 'jug cing dbang bskur ba'i cho ga.
123. rdo rje slob dpon gyi las rrim rgyas pa.
124. slob ma'i las rim bsdus pa.
125. rab tu gnas pa'i cho ga kun tu bzang po.
126. cha gsum rgyas pa 'od kyi sne ma.
127. bsdus pa rin po che snying po.
128. sreg sbyong don rab gsal ba.
129. thig rtsa 'od kyi phreng ba.
130. sgral ma mandala bz'i pa'i cho ga bde legs kun 'byung.
131. khri mun las thar pa'i cho ga yid bzhin nar bu.
132. 'jigs pa brgyad skob kyi cho ga padma'i dra ba.
133. 'phags ma dug sel gyi cho ga 'dud rtsihi ljon shing.
134. 'phags pa dyangs can ma'i khrus kyi cho ga rin chen nor bu.
135. rnam par rgyal ba'i cho ga yid bzin phreng ma.
136. sman bla'i cho ga yon ton phreng tshogs.
137. gnas brtan bcu drug gi cho ga gzhan phan nor bu.
138. kha 'bar ma'i gtor chen bar cad kun sel.
139. khro bo bcu'i srung bzlog gi cho ga gnam lcags 'khor lo.
140. gtsug tor cho ga bgegs dpung z'i byed.
141. dregs pa spyi'i bskang gso dnos grub kun 'byung.
142. spyi gsol chen mo.
143. phud rabs rgyas pa.
144. brnan yig chen mo.
145. bye brag ma mo'i bskang gso khrag mtsho khol ma.
146. gzah yi bskang gso dgra las rnam rgyal.
147. gnad sbyin dmar nag gi bskang gso ri rab brcegs pa.
148. dan can gyi bskang gso las bzhi lhun grub.

149. ma mgon spyi'i bskang gso yid bzhin lhun grub rnam dang.
150. bsyed rim gtsho bor bton pa sgrub thabs kyi skor la bla ma'i spyi sgrub dnos grub 'byung gter.
151. bye brag bi ma la'i sgrub pa dnos grub char 'bebs.
152. padma z'i bar sgrub pa rin chen khang brcegs.
153. padma drag por sgrub pa gnam lcags 'bor ba.
154. yi dam zhi khro spyi sgrub yang dag don gryi snying po.
155. rta mgrin dregs pa mthar byed.
156. phur pa sku gsum 'dus pa.
157. bde mchog yid bzhin 'khor lo.
158. 'jam dpal bdud rci 'byung ba rnams dang.
159. mkha' 'gro ma spyi'i sgrub thabs gser gyid dra ba.
160. bye brag gtsho bo rkyang par sgrub pa thabs kyi 'khor lo.
161. dpah bo rkyang par sgrub pa she rab 'khor lo.
162. sbrag mar sgrub pa bde chen 'kher lo.
163. gsang ba snying gi sgrub pa gnad kyi phreng ba.
164. yang gsang thod rgal du sgrub pa srong gi thig pa rnam dang.
165. phra mo'i sgrub pa la tshe sgrub bdud rtse'i bum pa.
166. 'c'i med dbang po'i phreng ba.
167. nan song sbyong ba lha lna'i sgrubs thabs zla ba'i nor bu.
168. rnan snang gi sgrub thabs nan song kun sbyong.
169. rdo rje sems dpa'i sgrub thabs sgrib pa rnam sel.
170. mi 'khrugs pa'i sgrub babs nan song rnam sbyor.
171. shakya thub pa'i sgrub thabs 'od zer kun 'byung.

172. byams pa'i sgrub thabs padma brtsegs pa.
173. 'jam dpal dkar po'i sgrub thabs shes rab gsal byed.
174. smra ba'i seng ge'i sgrub thabs blo'i mun sel.
175. ah ra pa tsa na dkar po'i sgrub thabs shes rab 'khor lo.
176. ser po'i sgrub thabs 'od kyi snang ba.
177. mi gyo dkar po'i sgrub thabs snying gi mun sel.
178. phag mo dkar mo'i sgrub thabs 'od gyi snying po.
179. ral gcig ma dkar mo'i sgrub thabs dga' ba bskyed pa.
180. dbyang can ma dkar mo'i sgrub thabs zla ba 'dod 'jo.
181. dmar mo'i sgrub thabs ni ma'i 'dod 'jo.
182. ku ru kulle'i sgrub thabs rin po che'i me tog.
183. tshogs bdag dmar po'i sgrub thabs nor bu'i bang mdzod.
184. rnam tshos kyi sgrub thabs rgyal mtshan rtse mo.
185. dzam lha ser pa'i sgrub thabs gser gyi khang brtsegs.
186. nag po'i sgrub thabs 'byor pa rgya mtsho.
187. nor rgyun ma'i sgrub thabs gter gyi bum pa.
188. aang gu li'i sgrub thabs ni ma'i dkil 'khor.
189. 'od zer can gyi sgrub thabs zla ba'i 'khor lo.
190. lha mo gzung kyi sne ma'i sgrub thabs dkar mo'i phreng ba.
191. dbang phyug gi sgrub thabs 'jig rten gsum snang.
192. khyab 'jug gi sgrub thabs grong khyer sum brTsegs rnams dang.
193. gzhan yang dregs pa spyi'i sgrub thabs ri nag spungs pa.
194. bye brag ma mgon lcan dral gyi sgrub thabs dus kyi mtshon cha.
195. 'jigs pa ma mo'i sgrub pa srog gi spu gri.
196. drag po gza'i sgrub thabs 'jig rten phung byed.

197. shan pa gnod sbyin gyi sgrub thabs ro langs skar nda'.
198. skyes bu dam can gyi sgrub thabs ging chen 'bar ba.
199. cho 'phrul gnam lcags kyi sgrub pa ltas nan 'phrul gyi bang mdzod.
200. 'gal byed khram la 'debs pa rgya mtsho du ru ka'i gtad khram la sogs te phrin las rnam bzhis bstan pa yun ring du gnas pa'i rim sgrub pa rnam dang.
201. nes don rdzogs rim mthar thug snying po'i don la sgyu 'phrul rim pa.
202. yang gsang thig le'i gnad yid bstan pa la. yang dag byand chub snying po'i rdzogs rim ye she 'khor lo.
203. bde mchog rim pa lna pa ni zab don snying po'i yang zhun.
204. gsang 'dus rim pa lna pa'i zab don 'od gsal 'khor lo.
205. sbyor ba yan lag drug gi bsdus don de nid 'dus pa.
206. lam 'dras bu dang bcas pa'i rim gnis 'khor lo.
207. chos drug gi snying po yang zhun.
208. bsdus pa 'od gsal rnam sbyong.
209. thabs lam zab mo'i don bsdus gsang ba'i de wid.
210. shes rab kyi lam rim sems khrid snying por bstan pa.
211. phyag rgya chen po'i lam rim gyi zab don rnal 'byor bzhi'i snying po.
212. cig car ba'i zab don thog babs.
213. dmar khrid gnis ka'i cha rkyen sku gsum don khri nam mkha' skor gsum.
214. me long bzhi'i gnas lugs.
215. sems kyi rdo rje'i glu.
216. snang ba lam khyer 'khor 'das kha sbyor.
217. rkyen snang rang grol zab dob 'dus pa rnam dang.
218. gzhan yang zhi byed don gryi snying po.
219. gcod yul gnas lugs rang babs la sogs paho.

(c) The Science of Metaphysics (Sunyata) section, consists of two sub-sections:

(i) General teachings of Vajrayana :

220. man nag rin po che'i rdzogs pa chen po sems nid nal gso.
221. de'i 'grel pa shing rta chen po.
222. bsdus don ni ma'i snying po.
223. chos 'byung shes rab gsal byed.
224. khrid yid 'khor ba dong sprugs.
225. rdzogs pa chen po bsam gtan nal gso.
226. de'i 'grel pa shing rta rnam dag.
227. bsdus don zla ba'i snying po.
228. khrid yid thar gling gsal byed.
229. rdzogs pa chen po sgyu ma nal gso.
230. de'i 'grel pa shing rta dri med.
231. khrid yid nes don sning po rnams dang.
232. sems sde spyi'i don bshad la. Byang chub kyi sems kun byed rgyal po'i sems 'grel ni ma'i 'od zer,
233. khrid yig nam mkha' klong gsal.
234. man nag gi don 'grel rang grel skar gsum la rdzogs pa chen po sems nid rang grol.
235. 'grel pa chem po 'od kyi 'khor lo.
236. khrid yid chos sku rang shar.
237. rdzosgs pa chen po chos nid rang grol.
238. 'grel pa 'od sne ma.
239. khrid yid chos sku rang babs.
240. rdzogs pa chen po mnam nid rang grol.
241. 'grel pa 'od kyi dra ba.
242. khrid yid chos sku lhun grub rnams dang.
243. klong sde spyi'i don bshad la, klong gsum spyi'i don bshad chings.

244. nam mkha' rab 'byams 'grel pa yang sa dog med pa'i rgya grol.
245. man nag gi don 'grel chos dbying rin po che'i mdzod.
246. 'grel pa chos dbyings gsal ba.
247. khrid yid khyab brdal klong yangs rnams dang.
248. man nag gi sde spyi don bshad pa la. sku dang ye she rgyas pa lhum grub snying po.
249. 'grel pa mi nub rgyal mtsham.
250. mtshan dpe sku gsum lag khrid.
251. man nag gi don 'grel kun 'dus rig pa'i gal mdo.
252. kun gsal snying gi don 'grel.
253. bar do ho'd kyi sne man la sogs pa zab cing rgya che ba'i gnas bstan pa lags so.

(ii) Instructional texts for the practice of Atiyoga meditation.

254. grub mthah rin po che'i mdzod.
255. rgyud bcu bdun man nag brgya dang bcu bdu'i don 'grel theg mchog rin po che'i mdzod.
256. lam khyer gnad kyi don 'grel tshig don rin po che'i mdzod.
257. chings nes pa man nag rin po ches gser gyi sgrom bu.
258. bye brag zab don snying por bsdu ba la. khrid kyi yi ge sems sbyong bdun pa.
259. sangs rgyas mnam sbyor.
260. khyung chen gshog rdzogs.
261. man nag gi lung rdzogs par ston pa bla ma yang thig yid bzhin nor bu chos sde lna bcu rtsa bz'i pa.

262. de las shin tu zab pa'i gnas bsdus pa zab mo yang tig chos tshan sum cu rtsa lna pa rnams ni bla ma snying tig byin rlabs lag khrid kyi skor dang. khyd par du smon lam lung bstan dang 'brel pa mkha' 'gro snying thig gi skar la man nag dus la babs pa.
263. mkha' 'gro lung bstan gyi bab lugs no bo lag khrid du bstan pa.
264. dbang khrid gdams pa'i mtshon tshul.
265. bying brlabs sems la shar ba nes don snying po'i gdams pa ste gnad gsum chos sde lna rtsa lnar gtan la phabs pa ni, mkha' 'gro yang tig hi chos kyi rnam grang no.
266. zhar la chos spyod las rim gsol 'debs drug pa.
267. snying po don gi mgur ro.

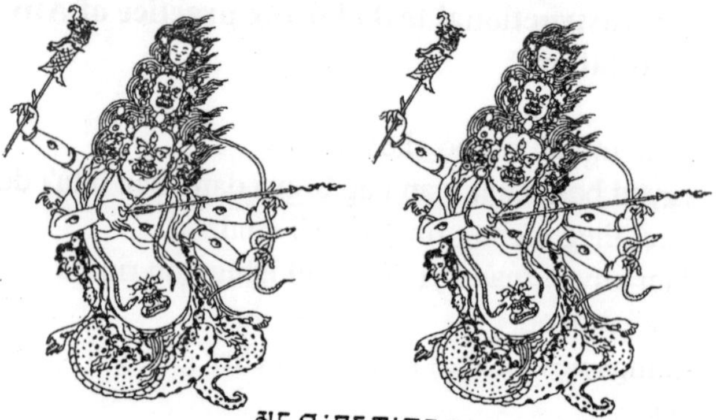

མངའ་བདག་གཟའ།

Generally, all the texts mentioned above are written invoking the protectors Ngadak Za (snags bdag gza), Damcan and Magoen (ma mgon) as assistants. During the composition of texts, his followers saw in reality that the great Gangri Chabjuk (gang rir khyab 'jug) was made to prepare the ink. Though these were the few texts written, people were not really concerned with collecting the texts or they were not even able to distinguish between the commentaries of the wise and foolish. As a result, most of the texts disappeared.

Throughout his life he authored a total of 267 works, only about twenty-five of which are still extant.

Therefore, to know about the texts the contents of the sermon called Rinpo Che'i Zoed (rin po che'i mdzod) is the final and last proof to enable us to appreciate the contribution of Guru Longchen Rabjampa in these days.

Likewise, the places where he expounded and sat exclusively for meditation to accomplish the essence of the meaning are as follows :

> Samye Chimphu (bsam yas mchims phu), Ugyen Dzong (au rgyan rdzong), Lharing Drak (lha ring brag), Shukseb (shug gseb), Gangri Thodkar (gangs ri thod dkar), Zhutey Tidro Yerpa (gzhu stod ti sgro yer pa), Yerlha Shampo (yer lha sham po), Bumthang Chambu Palgi Deding (bum thang skyam bu dpal gyi dge sdings), Gongpo Re'i Lawalung (gong po re'i gla ba lung), Kongpo Tsa Gonggi Phu (kong po rtsa gong gi phu), and others..

Usually he stayed at Gangri, Lhodrak, Ujor (dbu gyor) and at several places in Bhutan. Particularly in Bhutan, he gave Thri (khri) instruction many times to gatherings of hundred and thousand of listeners. He showed them an immense loving kindness and didn't collect the dharma tax; he didn't waste even a single grain of rice which he received in donation. To pursue solely the purpose of his disciples, he always bore heresy, sorrow and weariness. As a homage, he performed large sacrificial offerings; having read the thought of others, he used immensely skilful methods to bring them into religion. In brief, he achieved the stage of 'full comprehension,' Rangdon Pangtok Phunsum Tshokpa (rang don spang rtogs phun sum tshogs pa) i.e., he perfected his own purpose by abandoning what was to be abandoned and comprehending what was to be comprehended. Such are the practices of the great Kunkhen to lead gdul bya' (to be disciplined by religion) to conversion and salvation (smin grol), of emancipation by means of various desireless activities.

Some of his Chief disciples who appeared by perceiving the nectar of his speech (teaching) were:

<u>The three famous Buddhist scholars and holy men:</u>

(i) Zongthar Lingpa Khardrup Delek Gyatsho (zongs thar gling pa mkhar grub bde legs rgya mtsho),
(ii) Khadrup Chokyi Drakpa (mkha grub chos kyi grags pa) and
(iii) Khedrup Chabdel Lhundrup (mkhas grub khyab gdal lhun grub)

<u>The five spirituals sons</u>:

(i) Do Khampa Dengom Chokeyi Drakpa (mdo khams pa 'dan sgom chos kyi grags pa),
(ii) Gyalsey Zadpa (rgyal sras bzad pa) ,
(iii) Lama Pel Gonpa (bla ma dpal mgon pa),
(iv) Guru Yeshe Rabjam (guru ye she rab 'byams)and
(v) Zhonnu Sangay (gzhon nu sangs rgyas)

The four friends who propagate Dharma:

(i) Trulku Peljor Gyatsho (sprul sku dpal 'byor rgya mtsho),
(ii) Lopen Sangay Kunga (slob dpon sangs rgyas kun dga'),
(iii) Lopen Lodro Zangpo (slob dpon blo gros bzang po) and
(iv) Takgo Jadral Choje (stag mgo bya bral chos rje)

The four yogis:

(i) Phagod Tokden Gyalpo (pha rgod rtogs ldan rgyal po)
(ii) Naljorpa "Odzer Gocha (rnal 'byor pa 'od zer go cha),
(iii) Rigzin "Odsal Rangdrol (rig 'dzin 'od gsal rang grol) and
(iv) Jatong Sonam 'Odzer (bya btang bsod nams 'od zer)

(who closed the interstices in the above lineage and who attained perfection):

(i) Sangay Pelrin (sang rgyas dpal rin),
(ii) Drakpa Pel (grags pa dpal),
(iii) Lukhan Sonam Senge (glu mkhan bsod nam seng ge) etc.,

Drigungpa Kunrin (gri gung sgom pa kun rin), having become demented because of his own arrogance, was about to start a war against U-Tsang (dbus gtsang). Because of the seed of the flourishing virtues of his past, he encountered the prophecy of the great Guru (Padmasambhava). It read :

> *"In the direction of a land called 'dri ;*
> *The son of a devil named kun dga' will be born ;*
> *On the body will be a figure of a weapon ;*
> *After death he will be born in Hell ;*
> *From the direction of South, the embodiment of*
> *Manjushri will discipline him into religion".*

He examined his body and found a figure like a sword on his back. Having undoubtedly understood this reference to be to himself, he gave up the idea of a war against U-Tsang (dbus gtsang), thinking that it would be useless to fight if he had to go to the Hell.

Thereafter, he sent in and around Tibet to find the emanation of Manjushri.. Then, all scholars in one voice proclaimed that at present there was no scholar superior to the bsam yas pa (Kunkhen Longchenpa) in Tibet. He, having acquired full faith in the emanation of Manjushri, invited him and made him his Guru Tsukgi Norbu (gtsug gi nor bu).

At that time, he was treated in an unfriendly fashion by Ta'i Situ Jangchub Gyaltshan of Ü-Tsang (dbus gtsang), because he was a Lama of Drigungpa. By activities of limitless compassion, and by the Buddha's word, and by the biographies of saints and scholars, he became the Guru of Ta'i Situ Jangchub Gyaltshan too. Ta'i Situ was an Emperor of Tibet in those days. Likewise, Situ Sakya Zangpo, the chief of Ü-Toed, The Chief of Yardrok and Dorje Gyaltshan, and others, along with many other great personalities, paid respect to him as a Guru. Following the path of master Nagarjuna, the donations which he received from the above mentioned devotees were utilised for the purpose of the Triple Gems (the

Buddha, the Dharma, and Sangha). Once the necessities are dedicated to religion, it is not good to accumulate for one's use, it is also sinful to use them for other's purposes. He said that veneration should be given to the Triple Gems and not to sinful· persons. So he never showed hospitality toward any great personality. He believed it was not good to reciprocate the gift of offerings since the gift is the deed of a householder to accumulate merit. So he never returned any present offered to him. "Once something is dedicated to the Triple Gems, there is no question of give and take, however great the donation may be."[58] He had a great love and care for simple and poor beings. He used to accept whatever they offered heartily and uttered with urgency the prayer of dedication and recited the sutras for them.

Not only those who are practising these teachings (Nyingthig), but also those who perceive them naturally, i.e., by hearing or coming across them by chance, even those who inflict harm, are also supposed to go to paradise.

At the age of fifty-six, in the twelfth month of the Water-Hare Year of the sixth Rabjung(1363), he gave his disciples his spiritual testament, entitled Drima Medpa'i 'Od, or the immaculate radiance, in which he told them,

> *Having understood the nature of Samsara from beginningless time,*
> *That there is no essence in these worldly phenomena ;*
> *Now, before giving up this perishable body of illusion,*
> *Listen to this explanation of instruction, which is beneficial to one and all.....;*
> *In the presence of Guru Rinpoche, the protector possessor of mercy;*

Whom he held in every second of breath,
Like a guest who is set for his return journey after the arrival of the right time to depart,
I have gained the achievement of happiness at death;
The trader who makes his fortune at sea;
The rulers of the gods who achieve victory by war;
Those who decomplish Samadhi- my happiness is much greater than their's.
Now Padma lay-brel tsal will remain here no longer.
I go to dwell in the secure, blissful, and deathless state ('Chi med bde chen btsan sa).

Gyalsay Zoepa (rgyal sras bzod pa), having seen the testament, requested the saint not to speak like that and shed many tears. But the saint explained many Dharmas relating that all composite entities decay... Again, having received an invitation to visit Samye, he arrived at the Grove of Chimphu Pal through Jama (rgya ma) and Samye by performing sacrificial offerings. All these phenomena are like illusions and birth is like the Kaymo'i Tshal (skyed mo'i tsal) [bushes that were grown in the rainy season and last for only a short time]. The great Long Chenpa, having experienced all that, said that the place (Chimphu) was similar to that of the Silwa'i Tshal (Citawana) cemetery in India. So it was better to die there than to be born in other places. Having said that, he instructed that his body, which was essenceless, should be put there. Even though his body showed signs of illness, he didn't discontinue the teachings. Disciples thought that their Master was fatigued and requested him to stop teaching for the time-being, but he said, "I am thinking to complete the teaching before my final departure from this world."[59] On the sixteenth of same month, at Chimphu, near Samye Monastery, he made all his Dakas and Dakinis glad by grand offerings. Again, in an assembly of his disciples, he reminded them to strive for the Dharma alone, since there is no essence to material things. Furthermore, he gave teachings on impermanence, and especially on how to practice the meditation of Threk Choe (threg chod) and Thod Gal. He advised, "If you face any difficulties in understanding, read carefully the Yangthig Yeshin Norbu (yang thig yid bzhin nor bu); it will be like a wishing-jewel. You shall attain nirvana in the state of dissolution of all phenomena into Dharmata." He told them that he was going away from this world, i.e., to enter Nirvana (chos nyid zad sa la mya ngan las rdha bar 'gyur ro).[60]

On the eighteenth, he asked them to make preparation for a religious service and advised them to go away to do their religious devotion and work. But they requested him to allow them to sit in his presence. "Well, my illusion body, which is essenceless, is going to be given up here. So don't make any noise and stay in a state of deep meditation",[61] he said.

Having fixed his precious remains into the manner of sitting in the posture of the Dharmakaya, his mind dissolved into absolute Dharma space. At that time the earth shook and sounds were heard. His body was preserved for twenty-five days, and during those days the gods, who rejoice in the Dharma, pitched a tent of rainbows that arched constantly over the place, and flowered over it.

While relating the Gongpa (dgongs pa) teaching to Chos Nyid (Dharmata), even the great four elements got separated from their seasons. In the months of December and January the ice was melted by the heat and earth. The rose leaves started glowing. While taking his remains to the place of cremation, again sounds and rays appeared seven times. While setting up the fire (the fire lighted for cremation) his heart, tongue, and eyes fell into the laps of fortunate beings as a sign of perfection of 'Bodhi' in his intrinsic nature of the body, the speech, and the mind. As a sign of the manifestation of the attainment of wisdom,[62] the five kinds of Dungchen (large relics, or ring sels),[63] and many small ring-sels came out of the body as objects of homage for his followers. It is indisputable that the large lumps of relics multiplied by hundreds and thousands.

Even these days, it is generally believed that one who possesses a trifle of a relic without any damage will experience no harm from the evil spirits.

According to the Babluk Chenmo (a text about the successors of Dzogchen Lamas), Dra Khepel (sgra mkhas dpal) was regarded as a successor of the Dzogchen Lama by the earlier Lamas. But Long Chenpa said, "According to the serial list, it would be better to take Lodro Chok (blo gro mchog) as the successor of the Dzogchen Llama. There is nothing to be doubted even if there is a hundred years' gap between Kumaraja and the two lamas. On the other hand, they served the purpose of being in accordance with their circumstances and by manifesting themselves as the emanation of illusion."[64]

In reality, it is like the Kuntu Zangpo (Samantabhadra) who came to earth to turn the Wheel of Dharma. His Sermons, even if only four words, are esteemed highly by all devotees. Lord Buddha said, "Whoever explains or teaches the Dharma, to him I bow down with great respect." While explaining the greatness of his Guru and by praising him, Jigme Lingpa writes:

Although, possessed of the capacity of
knowledge, precept, compassion,
And like the two excellent ones and the six Ornaments of Jambudvipa,[65]
By the secret exercise of ascetic practice in holy solitude,
Long Chen pa passed beyond the transmigratory existence into Dharmakaya.
Thus, in every respect, I pray to the feet of Lord Drimed 'Odzer."[66]

NOTES

1 *rtag tu ngu, (sadaprarudita), 'Ever-crying'*; a Bodhisattva who used to weep while observing the miseries of mundane existence. His story is related by Sakyamuni to Subhuti in the Astasahasrika-Prajnaparamita-Sutra, Ch XXX, illustrating diligence. In the Sadharmapundarika, Ch xix, he is called Sadaparibhuta.

2 JGP3. fos.97b-98a.

3 JGP3., fo.98a.

4-11 See Padmalingpa's Ter-Chos.

12 JGP3. fo.98b

13.. *rdzogs chen sde gsum,* three classes within Atiyoga. 1) the mind class (sems sde), 2) the space class (klong sde), 3) the class of pith or extraordinary instructions (man ngag sde).

14 JGP3., fo.99b.

15 *Ibid.*, fo.99a.

16 *Ibid.*, fo.99a.

17 *Ibid.*, fo.99a
18 *Ibid.*, fo.99a.
19 *Hum* and *Phat* are a powerful and efficacious ejaculation used in mantras for the destruction and suppression of evil spirits.
20 JGP3. fo.99b.
21 *rdo rje phag mo,* (Vajravarahi), 'diamond sow'; adakini, she is the consort of Cakrasamvara. She and Vajrayogini are aspects of the same deity. Vajravarahi is marked by a sow's head protruding above her left ear. The sow represents Vairocana Buddha - ignorance and passion, Dharmadhatu wisdom and compassion.
22 JGP3., fo.99b.
23 *Ibid.*, fo.99b.
24 *Ibid.*, fo.99b.
25 *Ibid.*, fo.99b.
26 *Ibid.*, fo.99b-100a.
27 *Ibid.*, fo.100a.
28 *Ibid.*, fo.100a.
29 *Ibid.*, fo.100a.
30 *Ibid.*, fo.100a.
31 *Ibid.*, fo.100a.
32 *Ibid.*, fo.100a.
33 *Ibid.*, fo.100b.
34 *Ibid.*, fo.101a.
35 *Ibid.*, fo.101a.
36 *Ibid.*, fo.101a.
37 *Thig le, (bindu)*, 'seed-essence'; the essential fluid that courses in the channels governing levels of consciousness, as well as visionary experiences of drop of various-coloured lights.
38 JGP3.,fo.101a.
39 *Ibid.*,fos.101a-101b
40 *Ibid.*, fo.101b.
41 *Ibid.*, fo.101b.
42 sngags pa, Mantrika, a practitioner of Vajrayana.
43 JGP3., fo.101b.
44 *Ibid.*, fo.102b.
45 *rtsa ba gsum*: bla ma (Guru), Yi dam (Deva), mkha' 'gro (Dakini); the Buddha's three modes of being reified anthropomorphically, experientially they are indivisible.

46 JGP3., fo. 102b.

47 *Bardo,* 'intermediate' or 'transition' state, commonly refers to the transitional state between death and the next rebirth. One also speaks of six bardos: the bardos of birth and life (skye gnas rang bzhin gyi bar do), of meditative concentration (bsam gtan gyi bar do), of the dream state (rmi lam gyi bar do), of the moment of death ('chi kha'i bar do), of the absolute nature (chos nyid bar do), and of taking a new existence (srid pa'i bar do).

48 JGP3.,fo.102b.

49 *Ibid.*, fo.102b.

50 *Ibid.*, fo. 103a.

51 *Ibid.*, fo.103a.

52 *Ibid.*, fo.103a.

53 *'snod'* denotes man, in so far as he is susceptible of higher and divine things; a man is called a very pure and holy vessel in the ascetic language, Ja says.

54 JGP3., fo.103a.

55 These are the tenth day of the lunar month, dedicated to Guru Padmasambhava; the twenty-fifth, dedicated to the dakinis; the fifteenth and thirtieth, dedicated to Lord Buddha Sakyamuni; and the eight, dedicated to the Medicine Buddha.

56 Dam sri, Samaya perverter; a certain type of malevolent spirit.

57 The magical and powerful look employed by tantric experts in order to subdue demons.

58 According to Kunzang tenpa'i nima, in his lives of the incarnations of Pedma Lingpa, the singular characteristic of Long Chenpa was that he never acknowledged the importance of powerful people and only showed reverence to monks. He valued the gifts presented to him by poor, humble people. This was probably one of the reasons why he fell out with the Tai Situ and spent some ten years in a kind of self-imposed exile in Bhutan. The immediate cause is said to have been his desire to escape from the power struggle between the Phamo Drupa and Sakyapa factions, which threatened to involve him.

59 JGP3., fos.106b-107a.

60 Ibid., fo. 107b.

61 *chos nyid zad pa,* the 'exhaustion of phenomena in dharma', corresponds to the reabsorption of all phenomena into the absolute nature, which occurs simultaneously with ultimate realisation and represents the fourth and final stage of Thogal practice.

62 JGP3., fo. 107b.

63 The five kinds of wisdom are (1) chos kyi dbyings kyi yes shes (2) me long lta buhi ye she; (3) mnyes pa nyid kyi yeshe; (4) so sor rtogs pahi yeshe; (5) bya ba nan tan grub pa'i yeshe

64 The relics are mostly three kinds: relics related to the bodies of past saints, such as hair, bones, or clothes; relics related to their speech, such as pieces of their handwriting or pages from their personal books; and relics related to their mind, such as tiny pearl-like relics (ring bsrel) found in their ashes, which are the sign that these saints attained ultimate realisation.

65 JGP3. fo.109b.

66 Nagarjuna and Asanga are traditionally known as the 'two Most Excellent ones', while Aryadeva, Vasubandhu, Dignaga, Dharmakirti, Gunaprabha, and Sakyaprabha are known as the 'six ornaments'.

67 rdzam gling mdzes pa'i rgan drug mchog gnyis dang //
thugs rje lung rtogs mnam pa'i mthu mnga yang //
nags khrod dam par sbas pa'i brtul zhugs kyis //
'khor 'das chos skur rdzogs pa klong chen pa //
dri med 'od zer zhabs la gsol ba 'bebs //

CONCEPTION IS THE GREAT IGNORANCE
BY WHICH ONE FALLS INTO THE OCEAN
OF CYCLIC EXISTENCE;
ABIDE IN THE SINGLE POINTED CONCENTRATION
OF NON-CONCEPTION-
NON-CONCEPTION WILL BE LIKE CLEAR SKY-
BUDDHA

CHAPTER FOUR

TERTON PEMALINGPA : THE BHUTANESE' KING OF TREASURE-REVEALERS', THE RE-INCARNATION OF KUNKHEN

པདྨ་གླིང་པ།

To the east of Tharpaling, at a place called Dema Deng (sdod ma sdeng), in Bhutan, a boy named Thokar was born to Pema Cham (padma skyam) and his wife Lhakyi (lha skyid). At the age of seven, having gone to collect peas from the field, he was hit by a stone and died. Thereafter, he spent up to twenty-five human years in the Ngayab Pelri (rnga yab dpal ri) heavenly palace, sitting beside Guru Rinpoche.

Finally, the Guru commanded him to remain there no longer, but, "having taken birth in the world, and having acted as the master of my profound treasures, do work for the welfare of the sentient beings."[1] Thus, Pema Lingpa, in accordance with the Command of the Guru Rinpoche became a magical emanation.

As depicted in the treasure text *Rangter Sang Lung (rang gter gsang lung)* and also in many others treasures texts, Vidyadhara Pema Lingpa, the great treasure king, took birth in the lineage of Odsal Ngo ('od gsa gnos), from a father named Dondrup Zangpo (don grub bzang po) and a mother named Pema Drolma (padma sgrol ma), on the fifteenth of the second month of the Iron Horse Year (1450) at Chel Baridrang in the Tang district of Central Bhutan.

His mother's pregnancy was blissful and easy. In her dreams, she saw the sun and the moon shine simultaneously, and a turquoise-coloured girl carrying a holy vase descendend from the sky and entered the crown of her head. At the same moment, his father dreamed of a mandala that filled the sky, in which he also saw many wonderful events taking place. At the time of Pema Lingpa's birth, there arose three suns, flowers showered from the heavens and rainbows were seen. Even after the birth, for many days and nights, the baby and his mother were encircled by the light of a rainbow. Everyone saw the Dakas and Dakinis who, having bathed the Child, held him on their laps and sang and danced for him. He was given the name Peljor.

From childhood, he was looked after by his maternal grandfather, a blacksmith named Jangchub and his wife, Aunt Dondrup Zangmo (don grub bzang mo), in the monastery of Mani Gonpa (ma ni gon pa) near Chel.[2] While they were living there, Lama Cho Yingpa (chos dbying pa), the spiritual son of Dorje Ling (rdo rje gling), said: "Blacksmith, take good care of this holy child, and your son will benefit the Teachings of Buddha and all sentient beings."[3]

Pema Lingpa's activities as a child were beyond the activities of common children. Wherever he stayed he used to gather children and construct small models of chortens, thrones and temples. Thereafter, he would sit on the thrones, imitating the giving of sermons and initiations, singing religious songs and performing sacred dances; he often composed his mind to perfect rest for mediation. In the course of these play activities, he made many hand and food prints on hard stones, which can still be seen and from which we can receive his blessing even today.

Listening neither to his parents nor to anybody else, he used to do immediately whatever came to his mind. Therefore, he was given the nickname 'Dondrup Gyalpo', which means, literally, 'Lord of what he wants. Without any formal learning he recognised the alphabet; this definitely set him apart from what we know of all other Buddhist saints. Apparently he learned everything entirely by himself, without the help of any tutor.

Although he stayed at Rimocan for a very short period as a son-in-law of Lama Chokden, he returned to live at Mani Gonpa, in accordance with the last will of his grandfather.

The revealation of Termas

In 1475, when he was 26 years old, Pema Lingpa dreamed that in a cemetery, together with many Khandro (Dakinis) and Pawo (Dakas),[4] he was engaging in ascetic practise. And having risen to the summit of a nearby mountain, he saw the continents filled with light. The sun and the moon were shining simultaneously; they descended towards him from the sky, and he picked one up and put it in the pouch of his robe; the other he placed on his lap.

At the age of twenty-seven, in the Fire-Monkey Year (1476), he felt lonely and went off to look for mushrooms in the woods around the monastery. He found only a few. Returning, he rested and fell asleep in front of the monastery, nearby the congregation hall. He was awakened by a voice telling him to get up. As he rose he looked around and saw a priest wearing a ragged yellow robe.[5] Eventually, after much conversation, he gave Pema Lingpa a scroll of paper and asked him to look at it carefully. He then vanished. Looking at the scroll of paper, Pema Lingpa read the following: "During this month's the full moon night, take five companions and go to fetch your destined wealth from the rock called Naring Drak,[6] which lies at the bottom end of your valley."[7]

The next day he went down to the family home at Chel Baridrang. After explaining the situation, he showed the scroll of paper to his parents and a nun named Desheg. His father said, "It is falsehood, it is just a trick." But the nun said, "We don't know what it is. Such an incident previously happened to the treasure-revealer Ratna Lingpa (1403-1478), too."[8] Disappointed by the disbelief of his parents, Pema Lingpa began to lose interest in the scroll of paper, but on that particular night of the full moon five friends tried to take him to the site forcefully.

When he refused to go, they deceived him by saying, "We are going to receive a stolen yak-cow from the village of Tangsibhi." Immediately, after arriving near the rock of Senge Naring at Burning Lake (Mebartsho),[9] he senselessly shouted with joy and after removing his clothes, he plunged into the lake. There, at the Pelgi Phukring, the 'Long Cave of Glory,' he found a man-sized image of the Lord Buddha sitting upon a throne. To the left of the image were many chests of religious texts. A girl with a single eye in her forehead and wearing maroon robes picked up the chest containing the Text of the *"Kuntu Zangmo Longsal Sangwa Nyingcu" (kun tu bzang mo klong gsal gsang ba snying bcud),* which she handed over to him. After Pema Lingpa came out of the lake, he and his friends left for home, arriving at Chel Baridrang in the middle of the night.

He blessed his parents with the chest and took the text to Mani Gonpa. There they inspected the 'Yellow pages' with great care. At the very bottom were written letters in 'the writing of the treasure-teaching'. By using these key letters, Pema Lingpa was able to read the text as *Longsal Sangwa Nyinghcu,* the 'Quintessence of Secrets.' During the course of copying it, his ink ran out and it was replenished miraculously by the wisdom dakinis. At the same time, the Dakinis prophesied to him in a dream about a man in the Ura Valley who could copy the text.

The Lama Rinchenpel of Khabi village requested him to expound the *Longsal* text to a secular patron, as stated in the prophecy paper, and he decided to do so. But this put Pema Lingpa into something of a quandary, since he had no experience at all with the tunes and the sacred dances which were meant to accompany the text. One night, when he was worrying about this at Kunzang Ling, he had a dream in which the divine consort of Padmasambhava, Yeshe Tshogyal, appeared to him and said, demonstrating the sacred dances of the five classes of Dakinis, "Dance in this manner and chant each chapter in turn."[10] When he awakened, everything remained clear in his mind and he put all he had dreamt into practice and showed it to his disciples. The initiation and expounding of the text lasted for twenty-one days. Every night both Ugyen Rinpoche and Yeshe Tshogyal came to him to instruct him how to perform that part of the initiation and exposition which was due to take place on the following day.

On one of the full-moon nights, while he was sleeping on the terrace-steps of the Stupa at Dunkhabi, he had a dream of the treasure-revealer, Ratna Lingpa.[11] Showing great reverence, Ratna Lingpa said that he (Pemalingpa) had been his master in three of his former lives. He explained that he was now departing for the heavenly abode of Padmasambhava and exhorted Pema Lingpa to bring to full completion the welfare of sentient beings, Having said this, he disappeared. The next morning Pema Lingpa heard that the treasure-revealer Ratna Lingpa had passed away.

On the twenty-fourth of the same month, at the insistence of Thupa, the Governor of Chokhor, Pema Lingpa, in front of a huge crowd on the banks of burning Lake, holding a lighted butter lamp in his hand, took an oath : "If I am the emanation of a demon, may I die in this river, but if I am the heart-son of the [Guru Padmasambhava], may not even this lamp be extinguished and may I return after obtaining the required wealth."[12] He then leapt into the lake, holding the lamp. One after another people in the crowd cried out a lot of derisory expressions full of doubt. Suddenly, Pema Lingpa emerged from the lake, holding high an image of Lord Buddha, clasping a sealed skull filled with miraculous substances under his armpit, and carrying the lamp, which was still burning. The crowd was moved by this sight and its heretical doubts were washed away; among them this gave birth to everlasting faith in him. Thereafter, he was universally known as the great Vidyadhara Pema Lingpa, the emanation of the treasure-revealer. Soon after the treasure search, his followers constructed a Pema Ling Residence at Chel Tsansuri, and he stayed there.

In 1477, on a full moon day, he, together with his three disciples, discovered the *Thuje Chenpo Munsel Dronme'i Sam (thugs rje chen po mun sel sgron me'i bsam)* from the enclosed wall of Zangphu Dorje at Drak Rimocan in Tang District in Bumthang.

Later in the same year, in front of more than a hundred people, he extracted a small box of yellow paper and an image of Padma Guru [Padmasambhava] from the Lion shaped rock (senge 'dra) at the meeting place of two rivers in lower Bumthang. Despite the difficulties caused by great evil forces and a rain of stone, the sky was filled with a rainbow. At that time, he gave the blessing of the treasure to the public.

In the first part of winter that year, he made a trip to Kurelung in Eastern Bhutan. There, one of his patrons offered him a big copper pot filled with wine. Having drunk the wine to the last drop, he performed the miracle of the Nangsi Damnam Chenpor Tok, the comprehension of phenomena as great existencessness. He also extracted a vase containing nectar and the yellow pages of the *Gongpa Lamed (dgongs pa bla med)* from Drak Rimocan.

Returning to Bumthang, on the fifth day of the Monkey Month he extracted the Tadin Pawo Chikpa'i Ku and five hundred pills of Brahmin flesh from the Singey Nam Dzong Drak (seng ge gnam rdzong brag), a place where three rivers of lower Bumthang meet and where the lower ends of their valleys conjoin. Then, after erecting a bamboo hut on Serzhong (gser gzhong) hill above the monastery, he mad a three-month retreat, during which he had a vision of the whole world like a fruit of the olive tree placed in the palm of his hand. At Pema Ling, he expounded the profound instruction of the Longsal for a month. Then, on the thirteenth day of the winter of the Bull Year, he discovered the text of the *Tshedrup Norbu Lamkher (tshe sgrub nor bu lam khyer)* from Kurje Drak (Bumthang), beneath a cliff shaped like a pile of nine skulls. Then Guru Rinpoche, having come in the traditional role of Geshe, gave many teachings and explications of the 'Bardo' intermediate stage at Thayul Buler. In the Earth Month of the Dog Year, he extracted a bronze image of Buddha from the cave Gyagar Khanphuk (rgya gar khan phug), which looked like the stomach of an elephant, at Kurteo. He also miraculously left a footprint on the upper portion of the cave, which was so high that it was beyond the reach even of any pillar.

In the Dog Month of the 10th day he discovered the text of the *Drakmar Lung Khilpa (drag dmar me rlung 'khyil pa)* from the Singey Khilcok (seng ge khi lcog), in Bumthang. In the Pig Year, in accordance with the prophecy of Guru Rinpoche, he ordered the patrons of the Choskor to be more co-operative, particularly in religious service. There was a lot of amazement when he extracted a little quantity of gold from the corner of the ear of the Vairocana image to increase the fund for the restoration of the Choskhor Temple. On the insistence of the five classes of Dakinis at Pema Ling, he discovered a treasure chest of the Lama Drakpo Pawo Chikpa and an eighteen inch red bronze image of Buddha from Singey Khyicok in Lower Bumthang.

Having built the three rTen,[13] at Kurelung in Eastern Bhutan, he preached virtuous activities in order to accumulate extensive merit. On the 10th day of the Monkey Month, he took out the image of the Tadin Pawo Chikpa (rta mgrin dpa' bo gcig pa), measuring 16 inches, from Chaldrak in Bumthang, as signalled by Yeshe Tshogyal in his dream. While retreating at Serzhong, he experienced the dream-like illusory nature of all phenomenal existence and particularly, within one month, he apprehended the thought and deed of the six classes of living beings,[14] This extensively expanded his meditational understanding.

In summer season, having gone in the direction of Tibet, he discovered, in the temple of the Lhodrak Chukher Bantsha (lho brag chu khyer sban tsha), white-blue crystal miniature images of Guru and his Consort, filled with images of the white and red Bodhisattvas from within the crossed-legs of Vairocana, and also the chief of the five Dhayani Buddhas.[15] He also extracted the image of Padmasambhava from a rock shaped like a tortoise's back (the tortoise lying face downward) located at the end of the Mandala of the

Khari Gangul (mkharis' gang mgul). After he arrived in Bumthang, Daki'i Lung and Dorlek again insisted that he recover the Chest of the Kagyad Yangsang Thukyi Melong (bka' brgyad yang gsang thugs kyi me long) from Lhodrak, at the back side of the Tsilung Temple.

At the age of 32, on the full-moon night of the Snake Month, while sleeping to the west of his Pema Ling residence, Pema Lingpa, in his morning dream, saw himself riding on a white horse to the heavenly realm of the Ngayab Lingthren Zangdok Pelri (rnga yab gling phran zangs mdog pal ri), escorted by three girls.

There, in the midst of the wonderful residences of the gods, sat Ugyen Dorje Chang Maha Raksha (ugyen rdo rje 'chang ma ha rak sha), full of merriment, on a jewelled throne. To his right and left were sitting all the Indo-Tibetan Vidyadhara in rows, entertained and served by Pawo (Dakas) and Khandro (Dakanis). Seen them, he made a prayer and bowed down with deep respect and faith. He then had a long and jolly conversation. Going out for a walk, he saw many wonderful places, beautifully designed and well structured buildings. In a chamber made of five different kinds of precious materials, Tshogyal and Mutik Tsanpo arranged religious services and opened the mandala of Lama Yangsang Kadu (bla ma yang gsang bka' 'dus), which were performed for seven days. In those services Padmasambhava gave the consecration of the Jar (bum dbang) of life in connection with tangible substances (phyi rdzas); and the internal nectar of mystical consecration (gsang dbang), in connection with the 'Sherwang' (a consecration) of mystical method and wisdom; He also gave a consecration concerning the mystical identification of the words (tsig dbang), and the consecration of the Dorje Lopen (rdo rje slob dpon bka' rab 'byams kyi dbang). The protectors, having appeared in their own form, gave the vow and commandment forcefully. Having granted the benediction of the four kinds of consecration completely, Guru Rinpoche conferred on him a mystical name, Ugyen Pema Lingpa. After having listened to many profound Dharmas, prophecies and admonitions, Pema Linga returned home with the three girls, at which moment he awoke from his sleep.

In the Snake Month, at the insistence of the Treasure Protector, Pema Lingpa extracted the Lama Drakpo Pawo Chikpa'i Ku (bla ma drag po dpa' bo gcig pa'i sku), which was made from the sand of Mapham, the eastern of the two Manasarowar lakes in S. W. Tibet, together with the Drubkor (Sadhana), from North-East Singey Drak of Tharpaling in Bumthang.

In the Tiger Year, at the suggestion, given twice, of Terdak Shelging Karpo (gter bdag shel ging dkar po), he recovered the Guru Drakmar Che'i Phrengwa (drag dmar chen me lchei phreng ba) and the guide to Norgyam (nor rgyam), from the rock shaped like the palm of a hand turned downward, located to the left of the Kurje Dorje'i Gurphuk (sku rjes rdo rje'i gur phub) at Kurje, Bumthang.

Then, in main house of the Tashi Gomang (bkra shi sgo mang) monastery, he gave instructions in the generative and completive phases (bskyed rdzogs),[16] and he also gave the consecration of Sangwa Lamed (gsang ba bla med) to many fortunate beings. The gestures and signs of the activity of Sadhana, performed by Pema Lingpa, helped disciples in perfecting their meditation to attain Bodhi.

During a month-long mystical practise of Guru Sangdrub Ling (gsang sgrub gling), he clearly saw the Thothreng Rig Nga (thod phreng rigs lnga) in the whirl of a rainbow. Then, going to Chi Phuru (spyi phu ru) at the invitation of Phajo Sherab, Pema Lingpa gave crowd-initiation (khrom dbang), and the Phajo Sherab handed over to him a piece of stone for crushing a drug for blessing. Pema Lingpa thought, "If I don't make any sign appear on it, the people may abuse and generate wrong opinion." At that moment, having lost consciousness for a while, he made a clear handprint on a solid stone. In that way, all the people, changing what had been their wrong opinions, now placed their devotion and faith in him, and many of them came forward to assist him in religious activities.

On the 10th of the Sheep Month, at the suggestion of the Dakinis, he recovered the prophecies contained in the 'entrance certificate' (kha byang) from Kurje Drak.

Again, on September 10, 1483, in the presence of a gathering of the public, monks, nuns and religious persons of the Lhodrak and Troley Chung (spro gle chung), under the patronage of Lama Tenpa, he extracted a box containing the text called *Thukdrub Norbu Gyatsho* (thug sgrub nor bu rgya mtsho), a hundred pills of the Brahmin flesh, the images of the Taphak (rta phag), Two images of the Padma Guru, an image of Tshogyal, an image of the Phakmo on a peacock's egg, etc., from the rock like a tripod (sman mdo). Blessing all the gatherings, he placed them on the path of Namjang (Buddhahood).

As requested by the Nangso Gogo Gyalwa (nang so dgos dgos rgyal ba), king of Gaddu in Lhodrak Province in Tibet, Pema Lingpa unearthed a Sadhana of Tadin Cag Ralcan (rta mgrin lcags ral can), as a public treasure, from the huge rock of Drakmo Threng (brag mo phreng) at Lhodrak. He then bestowed the blessing of the treasure chest on the assembled public, led by the Nangso's father and son. The Nangso said to Pema Lingpa: "Oh great treasure-revealer, previously some people were saying you were a fraud, while others were saying you were truly a treasure-revealer. On account of doubt, there were few who believed you. It was for that reason that I asked you on this occasion to extract a treasure. From now on, people will believe in you and venerate you. From today you must also act as my root Lama. I shall trust you as my refuge in this life and hereafter." He continued, "You must go to Lhalung", so the Lord and his disciples left for Lhalung, where Pema Lingpa was received with all kinds of musical instruments and taken to the hall of the Great Chamber. There, as requested by Nangso, he performed the Consecration of Life (tshe dbang) for three days. At the end of the religious ceremony, Nangso gave Pema Lingpa an image of Buddha, one set of robes, one bronze cauldron, a horse and many other gifts.

Again, he recovered the dharma about Tadin and Phurpa from the left and right ears of the Singey Dzong of Mendo. While dwelling at Menthang, he rediscovered, in the presence of a crowd and as ordered by Guru, the text about the *Chakdor Tumpo (phyad rdor tum po),* as a public treasure, from Drakmardo. There appeared a great hailstorm and cyclone, but after performing an exhortation to the deity Gyadu Nakpo (gya' bdud nag po) it vanished instantly. Then, at the insistence of Gey Nyen Khari (dge bsnyen mkha ri), he recovered the Khandro Nelam Gyatsho (mkha 'gro ne lam rgya mtsho) from the nostril of the Singey Dzong and, together with it, from the eyes, the tantra Sadhana about the protectors of Buddhism. He then discovered an amulet made of wax from the rock marked as having a treasure, above the monastery of the Menthang Zalung. Since there was no prophecy about the time of its discovery, there were lots of evil forces around the treasure.

On the 10th of the Tiger Month, having been directed twice by the female protector of mysticism, he got a volume of text wrapped in the cloth [which was hidden in his previous life] from a side of the window of the ruined Chamber of Tharpaling, but most of it disintegrated as soon as he touched it. Then he brought down a set of the Gongpa Kundu (dgongs pa kun 'dus) texts. While dwelling at Pema Ling residence, on one occasion Pema Lingpa went to give the Consecration of Life (tshe dbang) at Lazhong in the house of the Patron Lama Chod. Having prepared the offerings, and while reciting the Going for Refuge (skyab su 'gro ba) and the Development of Bodhicitta (sems bskyed), their emerged a four-inch tall barley plant inside the vessel (bumpa). Then, at the completion of the generative phase (bskyed rim), it bore an ear of corn. At the completion of the invitation offerings (spyen 'dren), it turned into unripe barley (srus), and at the end of the life summons (tshe 'grugs) and the blessing (byin 'bebs), it appeared as ripe barley. Then having been roasted in fire, it could be consumed by all the people assembled there.

At the age of thirty-five, while going to Kurelung at Lhuntsi district, the Lord and his disciples camped at Drak Rimocan. In the evening, there arose doubts in the minds of his disciples that Pema Lingpa might not take them along for the extraction of treasure. Since they were unable to request him to take them, they decided to stitch closed the door of his tent and to sleep around it. Pema Lingpa, however, left the tent without being noticed and reached the top of the rock and extracted the Crystal Jar treasure, filled with Water of Longevity. On the top of the jar were interlaced peacock heads. At the time of extraction, a noisy sound of Mani (mantra) was heard. After the monks awoke, they saw Pema Lingpa flying like a bird from the top of the rock, and he landed on the top of a big tree. From there he instantly arrived in front of tent. While he was going inside the tent, he felt it necessary to remove the stitches. He bestowed the blessing by giving Water of Longevity from the Crystal Jar to all his monks, disciples and the public. Their lives increased like a waxing moon, and it also protected both cattle and men from diseases in the future. Even the crops were excellent. Thus, the sentient beings of Kurelung were placed into 'Mendrol' (ripened by consecration and liberated by authorisation). Apart from this, he also subdued all the evil forces on the mountains of Kurelung.

Then, having arrived at three villages in Lahok, he extracted the foot-print of Guru Rinpoche from Domtshang Valley. According to the meaning of the indications and the prophecy of the Dakini, on the 8th of the Pig Month he extracted a mystical treasure of a box made of Wax and wrapped in white 'Ga', by removing the dice-like stone from the middle of the three Chaitiya (Stupas) of Samye chimphu; after reaching Mani Gonpa, he opened the mystical treasure box and found: Twenty-five rolled papers of the Kunzang Gongsdu; Brahma Pema Karpo; from the closed mouth of the two skulls named Mukthreng Paley, Lhacam Pemasal's turquoise called Gungri Khamar of Lhacam; the Zichong Pelma'i Lentshar; the mirror Gyangsal made of silver; from inside the two Tshatsha of Sophak, the relic of the Jampel Shenyen; the robe Chogo Sergi Harican Gi Gongwa of Ugyen Rinpoche; the robe Zabdor Supmed Kyi Dumbu of Tshogyal; from the Yusar Gi Sa Tshatsha, he found a white and red Bodhicitta of the Guru and his consort. Apart from these things there also appeared many wonderful Damzey (religious objects).

Then he extracted a treasure box containing the pilgrimage list of Khan district from the first layer of a black rock that looked like a pitched tent, at Tashigang Tongshong Phukmar Khanpa Bong Nakpo (bkras shis sgang stong shongs phug dmar mkhan pa bong nag po) in Nepal.

At the age of forty, in the Bird Year (1490), while Pema Lingpa was at Lhalung, he was told by Geynyen Khari in a dream that the time had arrived to extract the treasure of the Phawang Yudron. "Go tomorrow to extract it," he was told. The next morning, he left for Monkhar Teng, accompanied by Kharpa Ponpo Dronlek, Chakchir Dungkor, Chushul Tokden, Zablung Trulku, and Togden Kunrin. After having prayed to the Triple Gems and given sacrificial objects (torma) to the Owner of Treasure (gter bdag), he entered a hole which was as big as the entrance of a rat, and from there he extracted a wax amulet sealed with six crosses. (The upper portion of it was marked with a hundred wheels. The bottom was marked with a hundred Padma, Lotus flower. The front was marked with a hundred Vajra; the right side was marked with a hundred gems; the back was marked with a hundred Padma; the left side was marked with a hundred Swastikas). Then, having replaced it with the five kinds of medicines and grains as a substitute treasure, he told them not to enter the hole, saying that it was dangerous. But Togden Kurin, the incarnate Lama of Zablung, and Nangso of Lhalung pushed their heads inside the hole. They were immediately struck by disease. The Tokden Kurin contracted leprosy, and the Nangso of Lhalung broke out in abscesses and blisters. Pema Lingpa managed to cure them. Thereafter they showed much more devotion and faith toward him.

On the 8th day of the Horse Month in the Dog Year, he recovered a bronze image of Vajrasattva, measuring sixteenth inches, its Sadhana, and the hundred letters of Azab Gya, from east of Tharpaling at the place called Shaja Drak.

Tangsibi Lama 'Odzer of Bumthang offered the Dzogchen Tantra Buchung text, 'The Little Son Tantra', which was earlier discovered by Terton Sherab Meber, to Pema Lingpa in 1490.

Although, Pema Lingpa took the volume to compare it with the original text hidden at Rimocan, the original had deteriorated so much that it was not of much use for sentient beings.

On 10th of the Dog Month, as prophesied by Guru Rinpoche, he extracted from the right ear of a lion-head-like rock at Rimocan in Bumthang a box made of wax containing a bronze Buddha image measuring 16 inches, together with a folded list, from the lap of the image as a public treasure.

In Samye, as prophesied by the Tibetan King Thrisong Detsan, he recovered the treasure from the meditation hall of Chimphu. From there he unearthed the Sadhana of Drakpo Thingka and sixty pills of the seven generations of Brahmin flesh from the legs of the cross-legged image of Buddha, as well as a folded paper of sacred instruction from the right arm pit of Buddha.

Though it was said in the prophecy of mystical treasure that in general he (Pema Lingpa) would be the owner of a hundred and eight treasures, for reasons of necessity he had so far extracted thirty-two great treasures, mostly in the presence of the public, as crowd treasures. Besides, he recovered some small treasure from Tsaldo Thraring Drak and Tsilung Gosung Nyinpo and others, from unknown treasure places. Those are not found in his comprehensive autobiography, but we know about them from his own treasure guidebook, Chotshan Thorbu. At that time he realised that the mind of the great self-begotten sky is not different, not separate, [from one's own mind].

The nature of the whole world of existence, Samsara and nirvana, is the Dharmakaya, primordially pure.
Having flown like a bird he penetrated mountain and rock unobstructedly;

He left finger and foot-prints on the solid stone,
as if it were mud.

At Kurteo Kunzangling, the residence of Kunkhen, he was carried by four Dakinis on a sedan Chair made of silk cloth. As requested by the Lamas of that residence, he opened the mandala of Gongpa Kundu and gave initiation and authorisation for twenty-three days. At the closing ritual ceremony there was a huge gathering of people who prepared a high throne with four legs. Having placed the sacrificial objects of consecration (dbang dtor) and Pema Lingpa on it, they stood in a queue to receive the blessing by passing under the throne.

In the winter of the Iron Horse Year, at Mani Gonpa, having been invited and escorted to the realm of Ugyen Dakini by four girls, he was given the identification of meaning by five kinds of Dakinis, Buddha Dakini, Vajra Dakini, Ratna Dakini, Padma Dakini and Karma Dakini; he was particularly advised by Ugyen Rinpoche. While dwelling at Lhalung, he also saw the palace of Khari.

Again, while staying at Nenon Monastery, established by Guru Chowang in Southern Tibet, the mountain god Khari invited him. From the roof of palace, Khari pointed out to him all the major heavens, starting with the Ngayab Ling, The Glorious Copper Coloured Mountain (Zangdo Pelri), the mountain of Five Peaks (Wutaishan in China, the palace of Manjusri) the heaven of Potala (the palace of Avaloketesvara), Alkavati (Canglocan, the heaven of Kuvera, God of Wealth), and the Akanistha ('Odmin) heaven in which Buddha was Vajradhara.

རྡོ་རྗེ་གྲོ་ལོད།

In similar fashion, Pema Lingpa had already met the divine Guru many times in his dreams and had received countless teachings from him; he was able to extend his cosmological horizons. In the very first of his extended dream journeys, in 1481, he was taken to the heaven of Padma 'Od, where his 'secret name' of Pema Lingpa had been conferred on him directly by the Guru. On another occasion, in 1501, the Guru had bestowed his 'symbolic teachings' (brda chos) on him through signs and gestures. The Guru's heaven of Camara (rnga yab gling) was usually designated the 'Happy Land of the Skyfarers' (mkha' 'gro bde lnga gling).

Moreover, the music and dance accompanying the ritual cycle of Pema Lingpa's first discovery was revealed to him in a dream by the consort of the divine Padmasambhava. The dances performed for him by the heavenly attendants in Padmasambhava's heaven were immediately put into practice. Later on he also performed these dances at the time of sacred instructions, at the end of religious festivals and also at the consecration of temples or holy places. Many of Pema Lingpa's dances are still performed in Bhutan with lots of gaiety and veneration. The texts he compiled, the dances he performed, and the works of art he commissioned are among the real cultural treasures of Bhutan to this day.

On several occasions, Pema Lingpa maintained that great storms of hail and wind raged after he had extracted treasure, and he managed to bring these under control by placating the treasure master spirits. At the end of his life, when his patron, the Nangso of Lhalung, used to come south, over the mountain passes, to meet him, Pema Lingpa several times ensured good weather on the road by commanding the spirits of the high passes to clear away the threatening storm clouds. His major undertakings, particularly those of a ritual nature, were always accompanied by unusual weather conditions: thunder resounding through cloudless skies, countless extraordinary rainbows, 'flower rain' and so forth. The whole of the natural world responded to his actions. In an injunction of Guru Padmasambhava it is said:

> *My spiritual son Pema Lingpa;*
> *Whoever will venerate with sincere devotion will be happy;*
> *Even the holders of heretical doctrine are not to take re-birth in Samsara; and*
> *Even tiny creatures are given guidance and protection by him.*[17]

In another text by Pema Lingpa, called Soldel Sungma he said:

> *Thus, by means of Dulja, (beings to be converted by religion) he had been to many places;*
> *And having made many consecration and demonstrated the efficacy of Dharma;*
> *Lead the fortunate beings to the 'Mindrol'*

(Conservation and Salvation) path;
He even prayed for the holders of wrong views.[18]

Some of the places where Pema Lingpa very often revealed treasures and gave instructions are : The four territories of Bumthang, the upper and lower Kurteo (Lhuntsi), Dungrang Lechung, the three village of (Lahok) Eastern India, the centre of Menlok Nyalja, and many other small villages. He had been to Lhodrak twenty times. He also built many monasteries, including eight important ones:

Bumthang Tamzhi Lhundrup Choling (Bumthang gtam gzhis lhun grub chos gling),
Chel Pema Ling,
Dechen Ling (bde chen gling),
Kurteo Kunzang Drak,
Bamrim Deki Ling,
Tsang Ching Ugyen Ling,
Layey Kerechung Tshitongye and others.

He also renovated Samye, Gyatsho Lhalung, and many other monasteries.

He then fulfilled the purposes of the four religious services, increased the welfare of all sentient beings and also prepared good omens to avert war.

Tashi Dargye, the hereditary myriarchs (khir dpon) of Ja district; the Karmapa Chodrak Gyamtsho; the Rabten Phak, the hereditary Governor of Gyaltshe; the hereditary myrarichs of Yardrok; Indian King dharma of Dongkha (Arunachal Pradesh), and the Indian king Kamata and others are some of the great personalities amongst his faithful followers.

The incarnate Lama Chokden Gonpo, Jangchub Lingpa, the incarnate Lama Zablung, Chógyal Wangmo, the emanate Lama Langlung, the Lama Shakya Zangpo of Drang Zowa, are some of the treasure revealers among his followers.

The ascetic Drukpa Kunley, the Lama Hayak Girwa of Jawanak, Tsang Lungpa, Karchen Kundrak, an incarnation of the female Bodhisattva Tara called Dechen Zangmo and many others are some of the Mahasiddhas.

Konchok Zangpo, Dawa Gyaltshan and Drakpo Gyalpo are the three spiritual sons of three classes of beings in accordance with the special prophecy of Guru Rinpoche.

The Lama Kung Wang, Lama Kun, Sangdak and others are the sons who will continue the family. The incarnate Lama Natshok Rangdrol, the Abbot Tshulthrim Peljor, the ritual chief Grubpa Kundu, Gyalwa Dondup the Nangso and others were the seven sons of the mandala holder. In addition, there were as many as 11,002 faithful followers.

Pema Lingpa brought down the Dharma (teaching) and showered the sacred Instructions, initiations, authorisations, consecration and grand ritual ceremonies on numberless fortunate beings in Tibet, Bhutan, and Northeast India. Scholars who wish to collect detailed information about the other welfare activities in which he engaged extensively and impartially can consult his extended biography. Here only a part of his deeds are mentioned.

Nirvana

At the age of seventy-two, in the Dog Month of the Iron Dragon Year (1520), Pema Lingpa made a final journey across the border to Tibet as a result of repeated invitations from his patron, the Nangso, and his disciples, and a special initiation from the Phakdor Tumpo ("The fierce Vajrapani"). The purpose of the journey was to give teachings that remained unfinished from a previous visit and to give the concluding blessings. After giving the initiations, he returned to Bumthang safely.

After Pema Lingpa's return to Bhutan, one day female devotees were offering cake and butter lamps in the temple of Choskhar and they saw the image shedding tears, and Yidam, the tutelary deity, bore a sad expression. Then all the passes and valleys were blocked by a great snowstorm. Some old people remembered how a similar storm had last been seen at the time Ratna Lingpa, the famous treasure-hunter, died in 1476. On the night of the November 10 he fell sick. On the second night of his illness, the public heard the sound of cranes above all the monasteries and the Lama's residence four or five times. Just before his illness, Lama Dawa, one of his sons, dreamt that a girl wearing a blue garment appeared and said: "The great Vidyadhara will pass away in the Snake Year."[19] Another of his sons, Drakpa Gyaltshan, dreamed of the setting of the sun for three times.

Finally, he gave his son, Drakpa Gyalpo, minute instructions on how to perform the last rites, saying he did not want a lot of weeping and lamenting.

On the morning of the third day of the first month in the Year of the Snake, at the age of seventy-two, just as the day was getting warm, he sat up straight, placed his feet in the lotus position and put his right hand in the mudra of counting the rosary. Finally Pema Lingpa uttered many sounds of "A, A", with his hands on the heads of his sons Dawa and Drakpa Gyalpo. Then his mind was absorbed into the Dharmakaya of Samantabhadra.

At that time, there were sounds of cymbals and flutes as well as many other sweet and pleasant sounds. Moreover, there was a good aroma that spread through the places he had travelled. The sky was filled with rainbows, there was a shower of flower rain and a thunder storm, and the quaking of the earth was seen and felt by the people of Dechen Ling and Kunzang Drak and others. In fact, these events started happening even two to three months before his death and continued for many days after. It was all due to the Vidyadhara's [Ugyen Pema Lingpa] miraculously going higher and higher along the heavenly path. As he instructed, they kept his relics untouched for nine days, by making offerings and saying prayers. On the tenth day they removed his robes. The relic of mind, as prophesied, dissolved into the Bodhisattva Dawa (his son) in the form of a one foot-tall blue girl. His precious relics still exist in the form of the Chorten (Stupa) at Tamzhing, for the welfare of all sentient beings.

NOTES

1. BNPK., fo.24b.
2. See Padma Tshewang, The Treasure Revealer of Bhutan, p. 41, n. 27.
3. BNPK., fos.25b-26a.
4. *mkha' 'gro ma*, Dakini; a very special type of female being who is capable of flying through space in her effort to be of assistance, especially to tantric yogis. More subtly, the dakinis is the practitioner's link to a reality which is spacious and full of dharmic potentialities. The femininity of the dakinis is linked with the symbolism of space or sky, the ability to givebirth or to actualise the full range of expansive potentialities. *dpa' bo*, (Daka); 1). Emanation of the chief figure in the mandala to fulfil the four activities, which are (a) milder worship, (b) abundant

service, (c) religious service to obtain power, and (d) terrific methods in coercing a deity by charms. 2). Male enlightened practitioner of Vajrayana.

5. Who in reality was none other than a manifestation of Guru Rinpoche.

6. The five companions were named 1). Guru, 2). Aphel, 3). Chobum, 4). Alek, 5). and Sonamphel.

7. BNPK. fos.28a-29a.

8. RSPL. p.35.

9. See Padma Tsewang, The Treasure Revealer of Bhutan, p.46, n. 32

10. *ibid.,* p.47, n.33

11 Ratna Lingpa (1403-78), a major Terton, originally from Lhodrak.

12 RSPL., p. 40.

13 The three *rten* are [(1) Dungten (gdung rten); receptacle for the relics of a saint (2) Chorten (mchod rten); stupa (3) Rigpa'i Ten (rig pa'i rten); receptacle of the heart i.e., the body]

14 Six Realms/Classes of sentient beings are: ('gro ba rigs drug). 1) Celestial beings (lha), 2). antigods or Demi-gods (lha ma yin), 3) human beings (mi), 4) animals (dud 'gro), 5) tormented spirits (yi dvags), and 6) denizen of the hells (dmyal ba).

15 The five Dhayani Buddhas are Vairocana, Amitabha, Aksobhya, Ratnasambhava and Amoghasiddhi.

16 See Gareth Sparham, Dzog Chen Meditation, pp.4-5.

17 nganyi thugs sras padma gling pa la //
dad cing mos pa'i sems can ah re skyid //
sems can se gu tsam yang lam sna zin //
zhes dhang.

18 gdul bya'i dbang gis rgyal khams kun la phyin//
dbang dang chos kyi 'brel ba mang byas shing//
las ldan pho mo smin grol lam la 'god//
log lta can yang bdul byar smon lam btab//
ces gsungs.

19 BNPK. fos. 229b-230b.

CHAPTER FIVE

RIGZIN JIGME LINGPA : THE HEART SON OF PADMASAMBHAVA

འཇིགས་མེད་གླིང་པ།

It is popularly known that the lineage of *Longchen Nyingthig (the Heart Essence of the Great Expanse)* belonged to Vidyadhara Jigme Lingpa, The Great Omniscient One. He was blessed three times, face to face, by Kunkhen Naggi Wangpo (klong chen rab jam pa), who was a magical manifestation of the three mysticisms of Mahapandita Vimalamitra.

In this chapter we attempt to explain, first, how the supplication of prayer was made by Guru Padmasambhava and, second, how the fruit of this prayer was fulfilled at the right time.

In the Central House of Samye Monastery, Guru Padmasambhava revealed the profound meaning of Nyingthig to his three spiritual sons.[1] By a great gesture of the Dakinis, the original instruction *Mar Thrid* of *Ku Rangjung* appeared from the chest of *Marthrid Longjang Neyik (mar khrid klong byang nad yid).* While doing this, they offered the mandala of gold, turquoise and especially the three doors,[2] to the Guru

Rinpoche. Then they made a request to Guru Rinpoche, who knew about past and present and could also foresee the future: "Now the time is auspicious and people are most fortunate, but at the end of five hundred years, sentient beings will be agitated by sufferings. However, because of your blessings we (Vairocana, Yeshe Tshogyal and Thrisong Detsan) are liberated (drol ba thob) from taking birth again and again; however, we would like to take birth in the future, in general, and at that time (five hundred years in the future) in particular, in order to turn the fortunes of suffering people and to bring them to Buddha- hood, after they have been reborn again and again in Samsara. So, we pray you to disclose to us in which place we, your present disciples, should appear? What will be the condition of religious activities at that time?"

This was a request, made at the Central House of Samye Migur Lhundrub in Tibet by the three of them, to Guru Padmasambhava to prophecy the time, signs, and other matters, concerning later appearances. Having made this request, they were utterly moved by faith and devotion in him. At that time the Guru Padmasambhava, having placed his right hand on Vairocana and his left hand on the forehead of Yeshe Tshogyal, and touching his head to the head of the Dharma King Thrisong Detsan, said: "You, fortune three (rje bang grogs), hear that at the end of five hundred years there will be a decline in the fortunes of beings, and the three receptacles will perish and consecration will fade.[3] After cursing, the Dharma practitioners will honour the sinful person. At that time the holy man of my emanation (i.e., Jigmed Lingpa) will perform religious activities for the welfare of others, as stated in the text *Kogyig Sangwa Lungjang (lkog yig gsang ba lung byang),* without any partiality in his generosity. At that time, by the blessing and

འཇིགས་མེད་གླིང་པའི་སྐུ།

prayer of the Vimalamitra, of Prince Muthri Tsanpo, and of you three (Vairocana, Yeshe Tshogyal and Thrisong Detsan), an emanation son named Rangjung Dorje Pema Wang will be born, and his mystical name will be Garwang Jigme Ling. By virtue of his being a genius, liberation will take place instantaneously. As a sign of his being a noble son, he will have a lotus eye (padma eye) in the centre of the palm of his right hand. Being a Vidyadhara of the speech Wangchen (rta mgrin), he will have the mark of Haya (rta mgrin) on his thumb. As a mark of his full comprehension, he will have an unoriginated letter 'Ah' (ཨ) on one of his teeth. He will have great compassion and sharp understanding. Because of his great wisdom, he will have little attachment to the material world. Due to his high knowledge, firm promise, and profound intellect, he will everywhere perform extraordinary deeds. He will be a fearless ascetic. Energetically, he will suppress phenomena by his luster. To Jigme Lingpa, the 'Thukgyud' (instantaneous reflective understanding) will come in the manner of the Ngoter or the Gongter.[4] Given the Consecration of 'Don' (meaning) and having met me either in dream or in reality, he will transform the blessings of Thukgyud, reflection. Then I, Padmasambhava, and Rigzin (Vidhyadhara Jigmed Lingpa), will become one cognition and one speech. And all the teachings of the Yanas will appear naturally in his mind."[5]

This was the prophecy about future place and sign made by Guru Padmasambhava, after he bestowed the prayer of empowerment to the public and particularly to omniscient Jigme Lingpa.

The second prophecy concerned the fulfillment in time of the results of the prayer.

Kunkhen Jigme Lingpa was the combined incarnation of Chogyal Thrisong Detsan and Vimalamitra. He was the discoverer of the Vast Ter or Treasure of the *Longchen Nyingthig* teachings.

Guru Chowang in his secret injunction concerning the text called *Khari Zhulen* said:

At the place of Chongjey, a boy who will
claim to be an incarnation will benefit
sentient beings.
People will call him Trulku (emanation) without knowing whose incarnation he is.
To the south of Ching bardo or Bangso Marpo
he may establish the Lhabab Stupa and monastery.

Moreover, the confidential...prophecy of *Gongdu* says:

In the south an incarnation named 'Odzer
shall liberate sentient beings through the
deep doctrine of Nyingthig.
He will transfer whomever is connected with him to the pure Land of the Vidhyadharas.

As clearly predicted in *Khari Zhulen* and *Gongdu* and prophesied in many other treasure injunctions, like those of Sangay Lingpa, Choling, Rawaton and others, Jigme Lingpa was born on the eighteenth morning of twelfth month of the

Earth-Bird year of the twelfth Rabjung (1729),[6] nearby the Pelri monastery to the south of Chongje Songtsan Bangso Marpo. From childhood, he remembered his previous incarnations, such as Sangay Lama (1000-1080?), and was motivated by a deep repentance caused by disgust at worldly matters and by unbearable sorrow at the nature of the world of misery (Samsara); in matters, he was able to see Manjusrimitra, Rigzin Jampel Shenyen, and others, in front of him, in meditation posture. They bestowed on him many teachings, meanings, and their accompanying gestures, which finally dissolved into Jigme Lingpa, which increased in him instantaneously his natural power of understanding. Therefore, his meditation became perfect, the karmical function came under his own control, and delusory appearance collapsed for him. Having strengthened his understanding by meditation, he almost forgot the existing forms of life and felt as if he had transmigrated into the next life. At that very moment, the persona of Nari Panchen (rna ri pen chen pad ma dbang gyal, 1487-1542) was recollected by him in an unclear form and he ended by assuming that same persona.

At the time, in one of his dreams, he saw the design of the kingdom of Sampa Lhun Drupma in an unknown place. In his human body, he saw the movement of a colourful heavenly body (unlike the human body in its physical form) riding on a dragon in the manner of Dorje Drolok (rdo rje gro lod). He thought it to be a Damcan Dorje Lekpa (Protector), but a man who looked like a monk appeared and said: "This is Ugyen Rinpoche, not Damcanpa."[7] and then he vanished.

When in the night of 25th October in the Ox Year he felt an especially strong devotion to the great Guru Padmasambhava, and on account of the recollection of the glimmering persona of his own previous life, in a sad mood, he thought that in his country, Tibet, the people were involved in killing. The teachings of Lord Buddha were like a shadow. It was a place where livelihood was gained by hatred and attachment, and where the people were wandering like orphans. Guru Padmasambhava, the supreme of all the Buddhas, had gone to the glorious Copper Coloured Mountain. At that time Jigme Lingpa was very depressed and was thinking about when he would be fortunate enough to meet the Guru. While still shedding tears, he fell asleep and in that very night he dreamed that he was riding on a beautiful white lion; he saw the limitless sky. After some time, he saw a village, and he presumed it to be Jarung Khashor stupa in Nepal. After reaching the path surrounding it, he went around a courtyard on the eastern side, where he met the wisdom Dakini, Choku Yeshe Ki Khandroma, face to face. After having given him a flat wooden casket, she said:

> *In the presence of the purified or fortunate retinue, you are a king Thrisong Detsan.*
> *In the presence of unpurified or unfortunate beings, you are a Singye Repa (yama). Keep this box well and secret, because it is the sign of Longchenpa of Guru Padma; it is the heart treasure of Kuntu Zangpo (Samantabhadra).*[8]

Then she vanished.

Thereafter, Jigme Lingpa felt somewhat intoxicated and opened the casket with great excitement. Inside were five yellow pages and seven crystal-like glasses. After he unfolded the big yellow pages, there arose sweet smells like camphor and other scents, all of which made him sneeze very badly. While reading each and every yellow page, the scents made Jigme Lingpa think for a moment that these pages were the proprietorial of 'Za', and he became frightened, because 'Za' was very strict and used to speak rigorously. On one of the yellow pages there was the figure of a stupa, on which were letters indicating *'Khandro Sangwa'*, which he was unable to read. When he was about to roll up the yellow paper, the figure of the stupa vanished, and suddenly, like magic, the mystic letters changed into Tibetan script. Now he was able to read and understand them to be a Sadhana of Avaloketesvara. So he discontinued the reading and thought, Who could be the master of this Sadhana? To whom should he give this? And what are the injunctions to be followed at the end of his life? Then, examining the footnotes, he found it clearly written that the Ven. Dodrup Jigme Thrinley 'Odzer, the incarnation of King Thrisong, should be advised to accept this religious property. Reading the remaining script, all the words' meaning instantly appeared clearly in his mind, like an image in a mirror. At the end, there was a word difficult to pronounce, which delighted him, and he put the paper and some of the crystal-like stones in his mouth. While he was thinking to return home with these yellow papers, a man dressed like a monk suddenly appeared as an assistant (who later was recognised as the protector deity Drangsong Chenpo and said: "I have thought from the beginning that such things will happen to you."[9] The protector deity Drangsong Chenpo showed great respect for him. By now Jigme Lingpa had arrived at the path around the northern courtyard, where again he opened one of the yellow pages and came to know the text called *Neyjang Thugki Dronbu*. The text was clear to his mind, in which it burst forth as the thought of consummate bliss. Since everything was clear to his mind from merely looking at its title, he thought to show it to his mother in order to improve her understanding. But while he was considering this, from the sky there descended a decorated

Lady, whom he indeed thought to be his mother. But when she came nearer, it was not his mother but a girl (Dakini) who explained the essence of things at Samye in Chimphu. When Jigme Lingpa showed her the yellow pages ('mthong 'grol', deliverance at sight), she said to him:

> *You always committed a fault by being happy,*
> *showing what was supposed to be kept secret.*
> *These papers not only liberated by being seen*
> *but also by being eaten. So, you, eat them.*[10]

By swallowing all the crystal-like stones and the yellow papers, the complete meaning of the words appeared clearly imprinted on his mind.

Soon after having testified to the efficacy of meditation, he rested in Dranrik Detong Chenpo (dran rig bde stong chenpo). At that time he saw various visions of purity, even in his sleep, and experienced, while asleep, 'Odsal Gi Kholor Jamley (od gsal gi 'khor lor 'byams klas).

The detailed account of these events, as well as a precept of his ancestor, are given in Jigme Lingpa's own text called *Chuda'i Garkhen (chu zla'i gar mkhan).* When Jigme Lingpa disclosed this account to his root lama, Drime Lingpa, the latter said: "It is the sign of an uninterrupted 'Ngoter' mastery of our holy lineage, and there is no doubt about the popularly of this Dharma, which is limitless in the manner of Daknang Gongter."[11] The Lama suggested to him, in writing, that it was very important to keep this secret from others, and Jigme Lingpa himself also realised that, since it is an iron age and most of the people were not aware of an instruction concerning treasure and its revelation and are in perplexity, it would better to keep it secret for the time-being, because it was not the right time to reveal it. Furthermore, if the marks and gestures, by which the *Khandro'i Sangzod Chenmo* (great mystic treasure text of Dakini) can be mastered, are not held properly, the meaning of the text would be lost.

Jigme Lingpa, who mastered these *Khandro Sangdzod Chenmo,* also realised that there are many saints who, because of their skill and intellect, claim to have reached the stage of *Daknang,*[12] but in reality are not as perfect as it is possible to be after mastering these texts. However, Jigme Lingpa was asked by his Guru not to disclose these teachings to others; but if asked by Dakas and Dakinis to disclose them, and if he were not to do so, then it might harm his deeds and life.

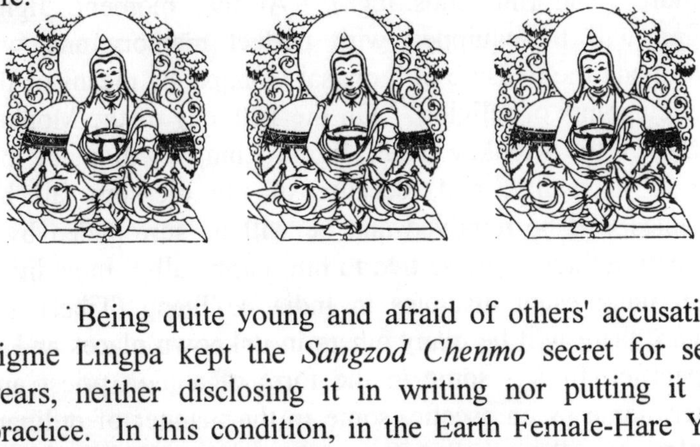

Being quite young and afraid of others' accusations, Jigme Lingpa kept the *Sangzod Chenmo* secret for seven years, neither disclosing it in writing nor putting it into practice. In this condition, in the Earth Female-Hare Year, while Jigme Lingpa was meditating Dzogpa Chenpo intensively for three years in the cave of Lhundrub Rangjung of Nang Phuk, below the Dregu Ge'u of Chimphu, near Samye Monastery, he understood, as stated in the tantra of Gronma Nampar Kaypa (sgron ma rnam par bkod pa), that from the transmission (tantra) of mind (dgongs pa), gesture (brda) and hearing (snan brgyud), purity or evidence of the meaning of tantra (dgongs pa brda' dang snyan brgyud nas; gsang snags don gi tshad ma 'byung) appeared. From the mere symbol of this text, he came to understand its meaning (dpe ia brten nas don ngo shes). Because of its unique character he had belief in it (rtags la brten nas yid ches 'gyur).

Jigme Lingpa was able to see Kunkhen Ngaggi Wang-po, the embodiment of Pandita Vimala, three times in the form of the Celestial region; Kunkhen suggested that he bring down the *Sangzod Chenmo*. Then, at the time of the 'Dradrol' of the chief of Dakinis, Jigme Lingpa, after classifying the treasure, started writing on white paper. The same event was mentioned in the text of *'Neyjang Thuki Dronbu'*, in which Guru Rinpoche said: "There will be three suggestions, by Rigzin (kunkhen), by Pawo (pra ti sngags 'chang) and by Khandro (tshe ring chos lnga). At that moment, Jigme Lingpa will be equipped with perfect memory and will promulgate the treasure of 'Longsal Gongpa' by means of the six viewpoints of religion.[13] On the 10th day of the Monkey Month of the Monkey Year, Jigme Lingpa will meet me, Padma, in reality; and, because of my blessing, all his obstacles will be removed and he will be surrounded by a fortunate retinue of those tied to him karmically. In addition to all the present disciples in India, U-Tsang (Tibet) and Bhutan, there will be many others in unknown places and in unspecified form - some in the form of a high priest and leader, some as an ascetic, some in the manner of ordinary people, and they will carry out various deeds without obstruction. The disciples will appear by Karmic power, and most of them will have a mole on their navel or on their chest. Particularly, due to the power of his prayer, the treasure door of Dharma will be opened by:

<u>Lama Prati Ngag Chang</u>, the incarnation of Nam-nying;
<u>Lama Tingzin Zangpo</u>, the incarnation of Nangben;

Lama Mon (Bhutanese) Jigme Kundrol, the incarnation of Chowang; and
Lama Drodrub Chen, the incarnation of Murub Tsengpo.

At that time, the instructions will be promulgated secretly.

As it was the Year of Monkey, in order to break the secrecy, Jigme Lingpa arranged a mandala of Ugyen Rinpoche and, having prepared various offerings (external and internal), he, together with his disciples, performed the ritual ceremony called Sampa Lhundrubma (spontaneous accomplishment of wishes), and the general prayer having thirteen secret instructions (Menngag Chusum). While performing the Chendren (invitation) ritual ceremony, the mandala, due to their unlimited faith and respect, was in reality transformed into the realm of Padmasambhava. A wonderful sight, with a rain of mandarawa (a red flower), was seen by all who were gathered there. Thus, he gained more popularity and fame as an emanation of the great Padmasambhava.

Now, after discussing the blessing of Padmasambhava, we will turn to the blessing of Kunkhen, which was made in three ways, (a) by body, (b) by speech, and (c) by mind.

(a) Blessing by the Body:-

This blessing, *Jinlab Dongi Negyud (byin rlabs don gyi ne brgyud),* was imparted by the great Longchenpa while Jigme Lingpa was dwelling in the upper cave of Nang Phuk Cave, which looked like a bird's nest and was where the saint Nang Tingzin Zangpo made a retreat. He lived at the base of a rock on which was a diagram of three stupas; the place was surrounded by bushes, which could hardly protect him from the cold breezes. On the sixteenth of eight month, after composing an eulogy about the place, he went to bed in the manner of the 'Odsal Drohong Mepa ('od gsal 'gro hong med pa) meditation and encountered a Kunkhen like mirage or image in the form of an adult properly dressed for the monkhood and looking like the Buddha. Kunkhen said to him,

Let the series meanings of 'thukgyud'
be transferred, transferred;
Let the series of meanings of words
be perfected and perfected.

As soon as Jigme Lingpa heard these words from the mouth of Longchenpa, he felt an irresistible devotion and respect and immediately held Kunkhen's hands and said:

O All Knowing Dharma King,
O All Knowing Dharma King,
O All Knowing Dharma King.[14]

As he prayed he almost fainted from faith and respect. Then Kunkhen said: "Finally there is a person who said that to me." Listening to these words carefully, Jigme Lingpa quickly understood this unhappy tone to be a lamentation, as stated in the text *Khamdu Metok Threngden (khams 'dus me tog phreng dan),* which reads:

Human beings are unlucky, because they
don't generate faith in me while I am alive,
But always practice or adopt heretical
observance...

Then Jigme Lingpa said to Kunkhen:

I am engaging in welfare and religious practices only by virtue of your teachings of the seven treasure texts (mdzod bdun) and the mind treasure (Kunkhen Yashi), out of all the Nyingthigs.[15] *So, remembering the kindness of your knowledge and wisdom, I have constant faith and respect for you, not less than that for Lord Buddha.*

Then, staring at Jigme Lingpa, Kunkhen said:

O noble son, by the way of 'Menlam Takja' (prayer) the series of meanings of reflection (mind) has been transferred to you. Now, do meditate and impart [these teachings] to as many fortunate beings as you can. The composition of your praise to Nang Phuk is excellent.

As soon as Jigme Lingpa thought of asking about some instructions, Longchenpa vanished. Now Jigme Lingpa found himself unable to remain without remembering Lama Kunkhen. In short, he received the blessing of the body and obtained the actual transmission of both the words and the meaning of the teachings.

(b) Blessing by speech:-

While Jigme Lingpa was residing in the lower cave of Nyang Phuk, he came across a treasure guide, written on the cave's walls by former saints; this was a guide to a cave to the south, which could be used for meditation in the future. He also understood clearly that this very cave was one of the meditation places of the Dharma King Songtsan Gonpo and King Nang. Therefore, at that place of great significance he also meditated. At the time, when he was about to free himself from a phenomenon always occurring to one's self which is taken for reality, he once again met the second Buddha, the all-knowing (Kunkhen). Kunkhen gave him a collection of books (dzod dun), saying that all the meaning of the teachings of *Shingta Chenmo* (i.e., Nal gso bskor gsum) would be clarified by them. Even, these books, he said, would also clarify Dra Drol (brda 'grol) of *Sangzod Chenmo*. Again, Longchenpa gave him a rolled paper and said, "It is a note from [one of] your ancestors (skye brgud lung byang)."[16] Unfolding it, Jigme Lingpa could see only two lines of letters. The first line read, "Your former birth was Kunkhen, the Lord."[17] Just as he was about to read the second line, it vanished. This time, Jigme Lingpa was completely unable to remember how Longchenpa was dressed and what he looked like. Having blessed him by speech, Longchenpa granted Jigme Lingpa permission to compose a religious commentary (bstan bchos).

(c) Blessing by the Heart:-

After a couple of months, Jigme Lingpa again met Longchenpa, who was in his mid twenties, in the form of a Pandita wearing a hat called Panzha Naring and leaning on a throne that was decorated with suspended ornaments and was situated in the centre of a marvelous mandala of Vajrakaya, by the sign of the spontaneous wisdom and method of the five Dhayani Buddhas (lhundrup Rignga Yabyum Zungjuk). He had a sweet smile and, without uttering a single word, Longchenpa gave him the empowerment of the 'Odsal Dakpa

Rabjam' meditational text. After receiving this blessing, he became the master of realization of the absolute meaning and all the forms or, in other words, he turned into a formless being (from rupa to arupa) and became a master of the series of meanings of 'Dongyud Tokpa'. This was the blessing made by the heart (thugs kyi byin gis brlabs).

At that time, all external images of essential phenomena vanished automatically, and his knowledge for composing his mind into perfect rest for meditation was complete. The grasping consciousness was pacified into pure nature. Thus, there was no disturbance at all of the state of mind of happiness and unhappiness in his realization of wisdom. Then, out of his enormous faith and determination, he composed a text called *Teypa Ciki Gyalmo'i Janglu (bstod pa dpyid kyi rgyal mo'i rgyang lu).* He also wrote down an oral instruction given by Kunkhen, referring to his understanding of the *Dzoddun (seven treasure texts)* and of the *Shingta Sum (nal gso bskor gsum*),[18] the *Pema Karpo*, the *Golshar Tsharcod*, and other texts, which are the essence of meditation on the secret instructions. He also wrote many texts, most of which have few words and but are characterized by lucid expression, intended to provoke 'Namlen' (aphorisms on things retained in the memory).

Jigme Lingpa believed that Buddhist ascetics who remain absorbed in deep meditation do not concentrate on textual examinations and expositions as their main work. The teachings of Longchenpa in particular were not like the religious commentaries that were handed down by those ascetics who had a deeper understanding of phenomena. Therefore, Jigme Lingpa thought there was no need for him to compose any texts. Even if he did compose some, he believed they would be almost useless, since there are more then two hundred and seventy texts by Longchenpa, whose value and significance were no less then those of the Lord Buddha, Guru Rinpoche, Vimalamitra and Nagarjuna. Because of his complete and through knowledge of the Great Treasure of Mind (kun mkhyen's dgongs gter chen po), Jigme Lingpa realized himself into conversion and salvation (smin grol) and, like the prayer made by Holyman Norzang to Bodhisattva Samantabhadara,[19] he also praised other gurus and himself promised to adopt the teachings *Gyacher Dompa (rgya cher dom pa)* and to preach them to others. In order to continue the tradition of the learned Holymen of the great knowledge holders, it was necessary to generate faith in the people and convert them into religious beings (Dulwa). For that purpose, Jigme Lingpa produced nine volumes of written and "discovered" texts: *Yonten Rinpoche'i Dzod* and its two volume commentary are his most famous works.[20] He collected the tantras of *Nyingma Jubum* in twenty-five volumes and produced a catalogue,[21] with full explanation, of their lineal history. He also composed commentaries on secret instructions, like the *Menngag Gi Tenche Rinpoche Lunggi Terzod (man ngag gi bstan bcos rin po che lung gi gter mdzod)*, which flowed through him naturally by virtue of his understanding of the profound meaning of the *Dzoddun (seven treasure texts*) as well as of various other texts and teachings. Apart from this, he also collected some of the *'Dorje'i Ne Chenpo'* (text of Atiyoga) from Longchenpa's texts. As Jigme Lingpa said in the *Tamtshok Le'u Redrukpa (Jigling Sungbum)* :

> *I didn't study the art or knowledge of Buddhist precepts but just met Gyalwa Longchen Rabjampa, and by the virtue of his speech and wisdom, I reached perfection. I have no pride in have reached perfection, and I would have not been disappointed if I had not reached perfection.*

Once blessed by Kunkhen, and having attained perfection, Jigme Lingpa felt that there was no need for the recitation of mantras or for ritual ceremonies. While he was in meditation, in other words in Sunyata, many relics appeared from his body. He made his retreat at Chimphu near Samye in Tibet. Because of his thorough understanding and realization of pristine nature, all signs and visions appeared to him as a religious book. In a cave, he gave for the first time the empowerment and explanations of the *Longchen Nyingthig* teachings to fifteen disciples. Then he prayed for the welfare of Bhutan and Tsang (Tibet). He used to pray meaningfully to all who came to meet him, by means of word, speech or mind. In the Donkhar valley south of Chongje in Southern Tibet he built a retreat monastery named Tshering Jong (the Land of Long Life). He did not want a big monastery and frequently quoted the verses of Longchen Rabjam:

> *To assemble a numerous retinue by various*
> *methods, to have a monastery with favorable*
> *accommodations, [all this] will come about*
> *for a while, but it distracts the mind.*
> *So my advice from the heart is remain alone.*

He made his dwelling place in isolation, as it helped him to keep away property (dkor) and vacillation (rnam gyeng) . His patrons and disciples used to come from U, Tsang and Kham. Ngawang Pelden Chokong and his brother, among others, and the king and queen of Dege province of Kham, became his chief patrons. Among his disciples were Dodrupchen Jigme Thrinley 'Odzer (1745-1821), known as the heart-son and the principal doctrine-holder of the *Longchen Nyingthig*; Jigme Gyalwa'i Nyugu; Jigme Kundrol; and Sakya Thrichen. He was supported nicely by the four kinds of alms.[22] Despite his desire not to be given gold, silver and wealth, from time to time they were offered to him in different forms. He honoured the Sutra, Vinaya and Abhidharma. He established monasteries or stupas and made many offerings to them. Then, by protecting the lives of sentient beings, he completed his life span successfully and also received the prophecies.

Nirvana

In the prophecy of Ugyen Chenpo (Guru Rinpoche) at Samye Chimphu, it was said that in the year of Rodus, in the month of Dusme, which means at sixty-nine years of age, Jigme Lingpa would pass away. But since he had not completed his work of Dulja (converted by religion) in this life, he lived for one more year. When he was seventy, on the third day of the ninth month, in the Earth Horse Year (1798), at Tshering Jong, in front of an altar of Magon Camdral (ma mgon lcam dral), he paid homage to the Buddhas and Bodhisattvas and proclaimed his dying testament by saying:

When I was born as a son of King Tri Tri (kri kri), I prayed to Kasyapa Buddha and became a younger brother of Buddha (Ananda). In Tibet, in the reign of King Songtsan, I became the monk Akarmati. In the early development of Buddhism in Tibet, I became King Thrisong-Detsan and built Samye monastery. At the time of Guru Rinpoche and Shantarakshita, I invited many Panditas, like Vimala and Muthri Tsanpo, [to come to the land]. Having performed religious service and worked for the welfare of others all my life, and by strictly following the practice of a Bodhisattva, I finally received the prophecy that I would become sanctified in the Buddha of Nampar Gyalwacan (Complete Victorious One).

Even in this life, without much hardship, he realized pristine nature. He understood all doctrinal systems without studying them. Since he spent most of his life in retreat and in delivering great loving kindness and compassion to sentient beings, he had no fear of death at all. So, while giving-up his aggregate form, he announced without regret that the time had arrived for him to go to the heavenly realm of Rigzin Trulpa'i Zhing and Pema 'Od. He said to his disciples:

It is not necessary to pray for me, but do you perform copious religious services to the tutelary deities, angels, and the guardian spirits of the ten quarters, as the main offerings at the time of my death. Since my body is no different from that of the flesh of the seventh rebirth of Brahmin, cover it with salt for one year and then put the whole body in a stupa. If this is done, the essence of the earth won't deteriorate. It will be useful at all times for the teaching of the doctrines. But there are also many foolish followers who don't take delight in me (Buddha), without knowing my lineage or connection with Padma. Because of them you may throw my body into the river. Don't perform a cremation unless you possess the right understanding of the Generative and Completive phases. Since there is certainty of a manifest emanation's rebirth, keep those religious articles without allowing them to deteriorate. It is not necessary to look for my incarnation . Apply yourselves to the prayer of Magon Camdral (Protector).

I am always in the state of Dharma; For me there is no staying or going. The display of birth and death is mere relativity (jey thob). Full Enlightenment is the great primordial Liberation.

A rolled paper was found inside his front table, in which he said:

I bow down to 'Odnang Thaye' Buddha. Birth is nothing but a wheel of life. Because of the continuity of the twelfth cycle of interdependent causes (Pratitya Samutpada), the disease and the like are the original causes of the truth of suffering. What we call death is ultimate truth. The entity of mind has no essence and it is only through consciousness that we classify what is birth and death. The understanding of the six senses and the full comprehension of the three doors of emancipation, this mixture is the heavenly realm of Rangjung Dorje. The Pema'od and Sukhavati or

Potala are excellent places to discipline sentient beings with compassion and loving kindness. Let the devoted beings who have connection with me achieve the Buddhahood in one mandala.

Having admonished his disciples with these words, he performed many miracles and finally, after having seated himself in the manner of the crouching Buddha, and after giving orders to make preparations for a religious service, his physical activities dissolved into Dharmata late in the evening of the third day of the ninth month in the Earth-Horse year (1798). His incarnations included Do Khentse Yeshe Dorje (1800 ?) and Jamyang Khentse'i Wangpo (1820-1892).

NOTES

1. The three 'spiritual sons' are Vairocana [rje], Thrisong Detsan [grog], and Yeshe Tshogyal [bang].
2. The three 'doors' are the door of the body (lus), of speech (nga) and of mind (yid).
3. The three 'receptacles' are the receptacle of the body, of speech, and of the heart.
4. *dgongs gter*. 'Mind treasures'; are termas concealed by Guru Padmasambhava in the mind-stream of the treasure-discoverer (*gter ston*). They are manifested clearly to the Terton at the appropriate time.
5. Ntg., fos.2a-2b
6. See Matthieu Ricard, <u>Thc Life of Shabkar</u>, p.xxix, n. 43

7. KSC., fos.2a
8. *Ibid.*, fos.2b-3a
9. *Ibid.*, fos.3a
10. *Ibid.*, fos.3b
11. *Ibid.*, fos.4a
12. *Dag snang*, 'Pure perception' or 'pure vision'; implies not only to respect the various schools of the Buddhist tradition as being authentic holders of the Buddha's teaching, but also, in a wider perspective, to perceiving the entire phenomenal world, including all sentient beings, as being primordially pure and perfect.
13. They are (a) dgong brgyud, (b) brda brgyud, (c) snan brgyud, (d) smon lam dbang bskur, (e) bka' babs lung bstan and (f) mkha' 'gro gter rgya.
14. kun mkhyen chos kyi rgyal po mkhyen
    kun mkhyen chos kyi rgyal po mkhyen
    kun mkhyen chos kyi rgyal po mkhyen.
15. *Dzod Dun,* The Seven Great Treasures:

    1. Yid Zhin Rinpoche'i Dzod, in twenty-two chapters, and its auto-commentary, Pema Karpo, and the accompanying instructions on the practice, Zabdon Dorje'i Nyingpo. Yid Zhin Rinpoche'i Dzod explains how to enter onto Mahayana practice. It provides a summary of the whole range of Buddhist doctrine, and it teaches the way of hearing, pondering, and meditating upon the doctrine.

    2. Men Ngag Rinpoche'i Dzod: a treatise using different series of six constituents to summarize the Buddhist sutras and tantras in their entirety, and to teach the essence of the Path and the result of Dzogpa Chenpo.

    3. Cho Ying Rinpoche'i Dzod, in thirteen chapters, with its auto-commentary, Lung gi ter dzod. An exposition of the deep and vast teaching of ground, Path, and Result of the three main categories of Dzogpa Chenpo, namely sem de, long de, and men ngag de, and, in particular, of long de.

    4. Drub Tha Rinpoche'i Dzod, in eight chapters: an exposition of the various philosophical standpoints of all the Yanas of sutric and tantric Buddhism.

    5. Theg Chog Rinpoche'i Dzod, in twenty-five chapters: a commentary giving the meaning of the seventeen tantras and one hundred and nineteen instructional treatises of Dzogpa Chenpo. It expounds a wide range of Buddhist doctrine, from the

way in which the absolute teacher, the Trikaya, manifests itself, to the achievement of the spontaneously accomplished final result of the practice of the Path.

6. Tshigdon Rinpoche'i Dzod, in eleven chapters: It is a summary of Theg Chog Rinpoche'i Dzod, explaining the crucial points of practice. It begins with a description of the Ground and concludes with the result, the state of Ultimate Liberation.

7. Nelung Rinpoche'i Dzod, in five chapters; with its auto-commentary: it explains the ultimate meaning of the three categories of Dzogpa Chenpo.

The texts of Kunkhen Yashi are Vima Nyingthig, Lama Yangthig, Khadro Nyingthig, and Khadro Yangthig.

16. TCZ., fo.16b.

17. *Ibid.*, fo.16b.

18. The three auto-commentaries of *Ngalso Korsum* are also known as *Shingta Namsum*, the 'Three Chariots'.

The *Ngalso Karsum*, ('Three Cycles for Relaxation') consists of three root texts, three summaries called 'garlands, 'three auto-commentaries called 'Chariots', and three instructions on practice totaling fifteen treatises.

1. Sem Nyid Ngal So, the root text in thirteen chapters: its summary, Kundai Threngwa (now lost); auto-commentary on the root text, Ngedon Shingta Chenmo; summary of the auto-commentary, Pema Karpo'i Threngwa, and the instruction on practice, Changchub Lamzang. The Sem nyid Ngal So explains ali aspects of the Path, beginning, middle, and end, of the Sutric and Tantric teachings.

2. Gyu Ma Ngal So, the root text in eight chapters: its summary, Mandara'i Threngwa; the auto-commentary, Shingta Zangpo; and the instruction on practice, Yid Zhin Norbu. This is the instruction on cutting the ties of attachment to existent phenomena through the method of the Eight Examples of Maya.

3. Samten Ngal So, the root text in three chapters: its summary, Pundarika'i Threngwa, its auto-commentary, Shingta Namdag; and the instruction on practice, Nyingpo Chuddu. This is the instruction on the profound path of Samadhi, the self-existent natural wisdom.

19. See Giuseppe Tucci, The Religions of Tibet, p.261, n. 11.

19. To generate faith even just one time may become the most excellence of the best virtue.

20. Yon tan rin po che'i mdzod 'Treasury of Spiritual Qualities' condenses the essence of the nine vehicles of Buddhism.
21. The collection of tantras of the "old translation," practiced by the Nyingmapa school.
22. The four kinds of *alms* are (a) Zang zing gi sbyin pa of gods, (b) Chos kyi sbyin pa of moral and religious instruction, (c) Mi jigs pa'i sbyin pa of protection; (d) Byams sags sbyin pa resenting affection, love.

THE GIFT OF THE DHARMA EXCELS ALL GIFTS. THE FLAVOUR OF THE DHARMA EXCELS ALL FLAVOURS. THE DELIGHT OF THE DHARMA EXCELS ALL DELIGHTS. THE DESTRUCTION OF CRAVING CONQUERS ALL SORROWS.

DHAMMAPADA

CHAPTER SIX

RIGZIN JIGME LINGPA'S SUCCESSORS AND HOLDER OF THE DZOGCHEN LONGCHEN NYINGTHIG LINEAGE

མདོ་གྲུབ་སྐུ་གོང་འཇིགས་མེད་ཕྲིན་ལས་འོད་ཟེར།

Jigme Lingpa, who is considered the founder of the Longchen Nyingthig tradition, was succeeded by the first Dodrupchen, Jigme Thinley 'Odzer (1745-1821),[1] who is looked upon as the principle holder of the doctrine of the Longchen Nyingthig. As Jigme Lingpa said in the text *Sangtam Chenmo (gsang gtam chen mo):*

> *Who will be the successor of this instruction ?*
> *To whom should I entrust this?...*
> *What kind of prophecy is to be followed at the end of my life? Examining the foot note of the same prophecy, it clearly says that Dodrupchen, the incarnation of the Royal Prince Murub Tsanpo, should be advised to inherit these teachings.*[2]

In a prophetic instruction from Guru Rinpoche to Kunkhen Jigme Lingpa concerning the Longchen Nyingthig teachings, the text of *Neyjang Thuki Dronbu (gnad byang thugs kyi sgron bu)* *state:*

> *The incarnation of the Divine Prince (lha se mu rub tsan po) shall open the door of the (klong chensnying thig) doctrine.*

In the text *Kaydzok Gomchok (bskyed rdzogs sgom phyogs),* Jigme Lingpa says that the incarnation of Royal Prince Murub Tsanpo would turn the Wheel of the Two Truths,[3] and by the innate power of Bodhicitta he would benefit religious work greatly. He was born at the right time as a result of the fulfillment of the prayer of the King Thrisong Detsan and Prince Murub Tsanpo.

Dodrupchen Jigme Thrinley 'Odzer, the reincarnation of Royal Prince Murub Tsanpo, who was the incarnation of Sangay Lingpa, was born into the Buchung family of the clan of Mukpo Dung in the Do valley of Golok in the Wood-Ox Year of the twelfth Rabjung (1745). The prophecy *Gongdu Kajama (dgongs 'dus bka' rgya ma)* of the great treasure-revealar Sangay Lingpa says,

> *Since childhood, he proved himself excellent and holy. He demonstrated various extraordinary behaviors like subduing the formless gods and demons.*
> *The ceremonial cutting of the child's hair was done by the Second Zhechen Rabjam Gurme Kunzang Namgyal (1713-1769?), who gave him the name Kunzang Zhenphen. He received teachings from about twenty Lamas including the Third Dzogchen Rinpoche, Nyedon Tenzin Zangpo and the second Zhechen Rabjam.*

In accordance with the instructions of the Dzogchen Rinpoche, he made an uninterrupted seven-year retreat at upper Kangthrod near Dzogchen Monastery, during which he concentrated one pointedly on sadhanas and attained high realization. While he was in retreat, his food was provided by the Dzogchen Labtrang (the monastic household). But after a few years they forgot to send him food for a long time, and he became very weak. He thought, "It would be better to go out and look for food. Otherwise I shall die, and that will be an obstacle to the practice." He arose from his seat and tried to reach the door, but he was so weak that he fell down in a faint. When he regained consciousness, he thought, "How foolish I am. My Lama instructed me to make the retreat, and to act according to the Lama's instructions is the main practice. To go and look for food will be wrong. Even if I die, I shall not leave the meditation cell." So he returned to his meditation seat, sat down, and resumed his practice. After a while, someone knocked on the door. At the usual break in his Sadhana, he opened the door and found a pot of curd, which he brought inside and ate. It had special properties which restored his health and helped him to develop his meditation. The curd was said to have been given him by the Dharma-Protectress Tsheringma. Since then, the environs of the meditation cave are known as Tshering Phuk. Some days later, the Dzogchen Labtrang resumed providing him with food. The pot left by Tsheringma, made of copper and gold, is still preserved in a stupa in Dodrupchen Monastery.

Dodrupchen Rinpoche visited Central Tibet four times. He spent most of his first two visits in Dhangla Ganpo, listening to the profound Dharma and making critical examination of religious precepts from a great saint, Damcho Wangchuk, and others. He also visited Kham twice, where he paid homage to Karma Tashi at Pelyul monastery; Gyurme

Kunzang Namgyal at Zhechen monastery; Drime Zhikong at Kathok monastery; Jepon Pema Kundrol Namgyal at Dzogchen Gyarong; Nedon Tenzin Zangpo, the incarnation of Padma Rigzin, at Dzogchen Rudam; and to many others great masters. From them he mainly learned the texts and commentaries of early Buddhism, especially Tantras.

At forty one, in the Wood-Snake Year of the thirteenth Rabjung (1786), he left on a third trip, this time to Central Tibet. His purpose was to meet and pay homage to Jigme Lingpa at Tshering Jong Monastery in the Yarlung valley of Southern Tibet. At that time, Jigme Lingpa recognized Dodrupchen as the incarnation of Royal Prince Murub Tsanpo, son of King Thrisong Detsan, and gave him all the teachings, like pouring one vessel into another, and he treated him as a father treats his only son. Then Dodrubchen was empowered and consecrated as the "principal Doctrine holder" of the Longchen Nyingthig Tradition, and was given a name Jigme Thrinley 'Odzer.

On Dodrubchen's fourth visit to Central Tibet, he brought huge offerings to the Lama Jigme Lingpa and received further teachings. At that time, in 1793, the people of Central Tibet (i.e., U and Tsang) were frightened by the intensification of the war between Tibet and Nepal. At the request of the government of Tibet, and with the advice of Kunkhen Jigme Lingpa, Dodruchen went to the Behar Kordzodling, the temple of protectors at Samye Monastery. Before the image of Behar he exhorted the protector, by offering spiritual prayer, to remember his vows; the image was seen to tremble and smoke came from its mouth and rose into the air. Then, quickly, he performed the Lhasang (Ceremony of offering of incense) on the peak of Hepori Hill; the smoke, moving toward the sky, was transformed into the dreaded shape of the garuda and was carried in the direction of the enemy, which was driven back. This miraculous event was seen by all the people of that province. Because of this spiritual power, he was honoured with a golden umbrella by the Tibetan government, as a sign of respect and a reward in recognition of his spiritual

accomplishment. Since then he became well-known under the name Dodrubchen, "the great Sage (Mahasiddha) of Do.

By virtue of his accomplishments and mastery of various religious activities, he subdued Jungpo Rolang (byung po ro langs), the evil spirit of the dead roving the earth. He was also able to direct the soul of the dead person into a heavenly realm by simply pronouncing the mystic word 'Phat' (ཕཊ྄). Once Jigme Lingpa, together with his two chief disciples, Jigme Gyalwa'i Nyugu and Dodrubchen, saw a dead body. To examine the power of their 'Phowa' performances,[4] Jigme Lingpa, after having covered the consciousness of that dead person with his crystal cup, asked Jigme Gyalwa'i Nyugu to go and perform the 'Phowa'. The latter saw that the consciousness was under a huge white mountain but failed to direct the soul into a heavenly realm. Then Jigme Lingpa asked Dodrubchen to do the same. He, too, saw a huge white mountain, but with his great meditational power he exploded the mountain and was able to direct the consciousness into a heavenly realm. Later, he disclosed the event to the Lama, but the Lama laughed and said, "You broke my cup, not the mountain." Such were the spiritual powers Dodrubchen possessed, equal to his Guru.

After making the pilgrimage to Tsari Rongkor,[5] Dodrubchen returned to Kham and, as prophesied in Jigme Lingpa's text, *Nejang Thuki Drombu*, Dodrubchen was crowned as a spiritual teacher by Her Royal Highness Queen Tshewang Lhamo of the Ga family and by her son, the Prince of Dege. He gave teachings, which included Earlier and Later Nyingthig, the Nyingma Jubum, and the Dzoddun, to the high lamas of the great Nyingma monasteries of Kham, such as Kathok and Dzogchen. Many disciples assembled from Mongolia, Amdo, Gyalrong, and Golok to receive teachings from him.

On one of the visits by the fourth incarnation of Dzogchen Pema Rigzin, Lama Mijur Namkha'i Dorje, to Drakchen Yarlung Pemakod Monastery, Dodrubchen asked Dzogchenpa to come to his chamber the next morning. Dzogchenpa went to see the Lama, as asked, but the Lama pretended to be sleeping in order to check Dzogchenpa's faith and purity of mind. Dzogchenpa bowed down to apparently the sleeping Lama without any negative thoughts. Then the Lama suddenly got up and said: "Oh! I slept too much," and he took a skull-cup full of chang (beer) from the altar and gave it to him.[6] Though he was a monk, he took the cup without hesitation, thinking that whatever the Lama offered would be a blessing. Immediately upon drinking the wine, Dzoghenpa was gradually able to realize all the paths (bhumi) and became competent in all the fields of learning, and he reached the zenith of accomplishment. In other words, Dodrubchen Rinpoche spontaneously transferred his understanding to him, whereupon he attained the state of Dzogchen realization known as "Chonyid Zadsa" (the dissolution of phenomena in absolutely pure nature). Thereafter he was a siddha.[7]

Dodrubchen Rinpoche recognized and prophesied Ngakchang Jalus Dorje, also known as Dokhentse Yeshe Dorje (1800-?), the son of Sonam Phen, from the clan of Golok A-Kong Chochukgyal, and of Garza, from the clan of Tsan, as the unmistakable incarnation of Jigme Lingpa. The Young Trulku was trained under his care and given the full teachings. Khentse Yeshe Dorje, becoming one of the greatest siddhas Tibet has produced in recent centuries, an adept in miraculous powers and foreknowledge, Together with Do Khentse Yeshe Dorje, Dodrubchen trained and developed many great disciples to promulgate teachings for the welfare of sentient beings.

As the "Confidential Prophecy" of *Gongdu* mentioned, among the many disciples of Dodrubchen the most important were the four named Dorje the six named Sangay, and thirteen others, also named Dorje. The four principal disciples named Dorje were:

1. Dola Jigme Kelzang, alias Chokyi Lodro, alias Kyebu Yeshe Dorje, a great teacher and Bodhisattva, who underwent death by torture in order to ransom the life of another person;
2. The fourth Dzogchen Rinpoche, Mijur Namkha'i Dorje (1793-?);
3. Dzogchen Kuzhok Gemang, alias Gyalsey Rigpa'i Dorje;
4. Choving Tobden Dorje, who was responsible for the spread of the Nyingthig Doctrine in Amdo, especially in Rekong.

One of the six Sangays, Chonyen Darma Sangay, spread the doctrine in Central Tibet. One of the thirteen Dorjes, Kilong Thuchok Dorje of Golok, possessed the Siddhi of foreknowledge.

Jigme Gyalwa'i Nyugu and Jigme Ngotshar were at once colleagues and disciples of Dodrubchen. Other disciples were the Third Zhechen Rabjam, named Rigzin Peljor; the first Zhechen Gyaltshab, named Pema Sangngak Tenzin; the Third Dzoghen Penlop, Kathok Siddhi; Kathok Getse Mahapandita; Chogyal Ngakgi Wangpo (a Mongolian king and teacher of Zhabkar Tshokthreng Rangdrol); Khedrup Tendar (1759-?), a great Gelugpa scholar; and Namkha Jigme of Rekong. In addition, when Peltrul Rinpoche (1808-1887)

was a child, Dodrubchen Rinpoche blessed him, gave prophecies concerning his future eminence, and gave him the name Jigme Chokyi Wangpo.

He turned the Wheel of the Dharma of the Early and Later Tantras of Buddhism, *Nyingthig Gong 'Og, Dzoddun, Rigzin Sokdrup, Kajey Rangshar Sok Janter, Dadnang Gyacan, Rigzin Yongdu,* and others. Very often he was blessed, face to face, by Lord Amitabha (mgon po hod dpad med). Again, as a result of the blessing of Ugyen Chenpo, all-knowing Longchenpa, Jigme Lingpa and Mila Zhepa Dorje,[8] he was able to "discover" many treatises known as "mind treasure" (dgong pa) and the complete the Min Drol' on the *Trulpa'i Kasung Mahadeva*, the *Choyul Chuwo Chikday Ki Kor*, the *Machik Labdron Gi Drubthab Wang Chihok*, the *Jetsun Mila Repa'i Ladrub*, the *Dzogchen Tenpa Chunyi Ki Drubkor*, the *Yangsang Tandin*, the *Nangwa Thaye Chinang Sangsum Gi Drubkor*, and the *Damcho Dechen Lamchok*, all being texts of "The Holy Doctrine, Excellent path to supreme Bliss", which were propagated in all directions.

Kunkhen Jigme Lingpa says in his *autobiography*,

> *Dola [Lama of Do, meaning Dodrubchen] has given the explanatory teachings of Nyingthig (in Dege) three times. On the first occasion two thousand disciples received teachings; On the second, three thousand, and on the third five thousand.*
>
> *Many lay people took vows against hunting, whereby many sentient beings received 'the gift of fearlessness.' I feel happy that I have caused this small result by staying in a remote place and developing the actualization of Bodhicitta.*

He founded two monasteries in the upper and lower Dzagyud to impart and maintain the religious order of Kunkhen; the lower Dzagyud later became the seat of Jigme Gyalwa'i Nyugu and his disciple, Peltrul Rinpoche.

In his treasure prophecy, Rongten Dechenlingpa says:

> *An incarnation of the Royal Prince Murub Tsanpo, heroic Bodhisattva, will appear, a teacher of a group of Dzogchen Ati-Meditators. He will establish about three monasteries in upper, middle, and lower Ser valley.*

Fulfilling the prophecy, he established Drodon Lhundrub Monastery at Shukchen Takgo in the Do valley. His colleague and disciple Jigme Gyalwa'i Nyugu acted as manager for the building of the monastery. Before long, Dodrubchen abandoned this monastery and built Padma bkod rtsa-gsum mkha' 'gro'i-ling Monastery in Drakchen Yarlung Valley. There people still can hear the beating of bells, the striking of cymbals and the musical sound of chanting, performed by the assembly of Pawo (Dakas) and Khandro (dakinis) on the tenth and twenty-fifth days of the Lunar calendar. Listening to these musical sounds, the people remember to commemorate the auspicious tenth and twenty-fifth day of each lunar calendar. Because of such an extraordinary blessing, a nice scent can be discerned even far from the monastery. Nearby, there is a great cremation ground, which is praised as resembling the Silwatshal cremation ground in India. The greatness of this cremation ground can be realized from the fact that Kangka Rozan, the bird of cremation grounds, arrives there from time to time. Moreover, the cremation stone, which is as big as the head of a man, looks like a water-pot. It is characteristic of this cremation stone that if it is rolled down to the lower part of the valley today, it will return to its original place tomorrow, with nobody's help. It was at this wonderful place that Dodrubchen spent the rest of his life.

To the north of this monastery, on the bank of the Machu Karmo Jakhil River, the A-Ring Ragya monastery of the Gelukpa school was built. On one occasion, due to the reverse of earlier omens and due to calamitous evil forces of an epidemic spread in the monastery and some half of the four-thousand monks died. Being unable to stay there, the followers of the Gelukpa sect pitched their tents on the left side of their monastery and stayed there. Later, that valley was known as the Garlung (valley of tents). A priest who was in charge of a Chapel of Maitreya Buddha scarified his life by not moving away from the monastery, he stayed there to perform the daily service to the deities. One day, having heard the sound of a bell outside the chapel, he looked out and, to his surprise, saw a man (discovered later to have been Dodrubchen), looking like a farmer riding on a tiger decorated with small bells around his neck. The priest said to Dodrubchen, "Your coming here is not good."[9] As the priest narrated the whole story of the incident caused by the epidemic, Dodrubchen displayed miraculous signs and performed a fire ceremony (hom), which stopped the epidemic and enabled the survivors to return to the monastery.

ཨེ་ཀ་ཛ་ཏི།

He drew out a miraculous stream of water from A-Mye Chungon, the rocky mountain behind the monastery. He stayed for a long time in a recess there and performed services and worship. The stream formed a wonderful lake which still exists and is an object of respect. Then, going towards Rekong (Amdo), he bestowed 'Min Drol' and became the master of one thousand and nine hundred Tantikas, who were even able to fly. He was reverenced for a long time as a spiritual teacher by the Yogpo Bang ("Brilliant King") of the Koko Nor region of Mongolia. Then Dodrubchen presented a volume of books of future prophecies to the king; this volume was later attested to be the main religious object of Ladrang Tashi Gomang ("the stupa with many doors"). Because of his all-pervading accomplishments and foreknowledge, many disciples from the upper and lower Dokhams, India, China, Bhutan, Turkestan, Gyalrong, Dardo as well as other great personalities, gathered around him like a cloud.

Through his teaching of non-violence and loving kindness, he helped the religious and political bodies to uplift their activities in an environment of harmony. Having accomplished all this, at the age of seventy-seven, on the thirteen day of the first month of the Iron-Snake Year (1821), without any sign of illness, he gave instructions to his disciples individually and explained the phases of the withdrawal of energy from the body at the time of death. Then he entered into Nirvana amidst miraculous signs. When his body was cremated, many Ringsel (relics) emerged, and his followers built a golden stupa in which they preserved his remains. The stupa of his relics still exists for the well-being of others.

NOTES

1. See Mattieu Ricard, The Life of Shabkar, p.xxix, n. 48.
2. See Chapter V. p.8.
3. *bden pa gnyis,* Two truths; Absolute truth and relative truth. Absolute truth (bden pa) is don dam beyond concepts and definitions. Relative truth (Kun rdzob bden pa) is considered as

deceptive and devoid of any true existence; or, according to the Mantrayana, as the display of innate wisdom, the infinite purity of all phenomena.

4. *Phowa;* the transference of consciousness, at the moment of death, to a Buddhafield where Buddhahood will ultimately be attained. The Phowa should be performed for the dying person only when the outer life-wind is stopped and the inner wind is about to depart, otherwise it will have no effect at all. It is like a guest who has set out on an unknown journey and is guided by a friend. There is also a practice known as "phowa for living" (gson 'pho) or "phowa transmission" ('pho lung) in which the method of the transference of the consciousness to a Buddhafield may be given, in association with a blessing to attract longevity (tshe 'gugs), to old persons before their death.

5. See Matthieu Ricard, The Life of Shabkar, p.267 n. 1.

6. He purposely had put, the skull-cup of beer on a altar before going to bed in order to it give to Dzogchenpa, the following morning.

7. *Grub thob,* Siddha 'accomplished one'; a term for an enlightened master in the tantric tradition. i.e., one who makes no distinctions between, and who has no hope or fear of , good and bad. Tilopa, Naropa, and Maitripa are among the famed eighty-four Mahasiddhas.

8. Jetsun Milarepa or Mila Zhepa Dorje ('laughing Vajra', rje btsun mi la ras pa bzhad pa'i rdo rje, 1040-1123), the most famous of all Tibetan ascetics. Disciple of Marpa Lotsawa, the father of the Kagyu lineage, he was the archetype of the perfect disciple, practitioner, and teacher.

9. DEH.,fo.7a.

I SHOW YOU THE WAY TO LIBERATION,
BUT KNOW THAT LIBERATION REST WITH YOU.
BUDDHA

Padmasambhava

CONCLUSION

The *Lion of Sakyas* is the only one who has guided sentient beings in their temporal and ultimate state of life.

In the glorious period, i.e., about the 3rd century B.C.E., Buddha taught the people disciplined and performed welfare functions in his true physical presence. In the following period he accomplished the same tasks by emanating through various *panditas* and *Arhats*. They made a collection of the Buddha's teachings and organized a Buddhist Council to continue the process of collecting and promulgating the precepts of the Buddha.

Even today, in order to preserve the teachings and to show the path of liberation to sentient beings, Buddha continues to take embodiment in the "spiritual companions" *(Kalyanmitra).* In the *Mahaparinirvana* and *Ngawog Chepo (nga bo chen po)* sutras, the Buddha, at the time of Nirvana, said to his cousin Ananda: " Ananda (kun dga' bo), don't lament; Ananda, don't bewail; in the future I, having emanated in spiritual companions, will appear to benefit you and others."

(mya ngan ma byed kun dga' bo;
smre sngas ma 'don kun dga' bo;
nga ni phyi ma'i dus kyi tshe;
dge ba'i bshes gnyen nyid sprul nas;
khyod la sogs pa'i don du 'gyur).

In accordance with his promise to Ananda, Buddha has emanated from time to time in various spiritual Gurus. In the present, degenerate, era, when Dharma and life have declined, these spiritual Gurus have been emanating In various spiritual companions and are enlightening the people by showing them the path of Buddhahood.

Among such emanations Guru Padmasambhava, the second Buddha, is the supreme. In the *Ausgyur Lungten (dbus dgyur lung bstan)* sutra, Buddha foretold that he would be born in a lake. This prophecy was fulfilled by the 'Lotus born,' Padmasambhava, who was born from a lotus in a lake. He said:

> " At the time of Zhisum Chuni, (after twelve years);
> from the unpolluted Pedma (lotus) of Kosha lake,
> will appear the holy prince of king Indrabodhi and
> he will turn the wheel of *Dharma of Lamed Nyingpo*
> *(bla med snying po)*
> *(rtag lta sun 'byin nga ni mya ngan 'das;*
> *chad lta sun 'byin bzhi gsum bcu gnyis na;*
> *ko sha'i mtsho gling dri med pedma las;*
> *rgyal po thugs rgyes sras kyi dam por 'gyur;*
> *bla med snying po don gi chos 'khor bskor;).*

Thus Guru Padmasambhava, who was praised by many different "conquerors" (rgyal ba), manifested different forms and subdued evil spirits and heretics in all the directions of India, and he propagated the Buddha Dharma extensively. He also gave various kinds of teachings, and many of his disciples reached *sidhis (dngos grub),* which resulted only from the successful practice of meditation and yoga.

Buddha Dharma also originated in Tibet. In accordance with Buddha's sutra *'Lhamo Drima Medpa,* Buddha foretold, "After my Mahaparinirvana, the teachings of Dharma will develop in the place called Dongmarchan (gdong dmar can), i.e.,Tibet.

ཏྲི་སྟེ།

Because of Buddha's prophecy, together with the supreme supplication and selfless devotion of Padmasambhava, Santaraksita and King Thrisong Detshan, and the selfless service of many other great scholars and holy men, the teachings of Buddha flourished in the "dark land of snows," that is, in Tibet and Bhutan.

Padmasambhava, having created twenty-five main *Mahasiddhas* and many other Mahasiddhas as well, exhibited successive miracles which made the " fortunate beings"(bdul bya*)* realize the knowledge of reality in their own minds. In later times, various embodiments of the great treasure revealers, such as Pema Lingpa, appeared and fulfilled the needs of the people through their selfless services. They became a great boon to us. *Tolmed Dzogpa Chenpo (rtol med rdzogs pa chen po),* particularly, is the essence and pith of all the Dharma of all the Buddhas, and it is even beyond all the nine *yanas*. By perceiving just the root meaning of *Nyingthig,* the teaching of Dzogchen, the projection of our view and meditation are no longer needed; without any hardship we can complete the Bhumis and paths (sa lam); without spiritual knowledge and artificial modification, one can gain freedom from ignorance. The very significance of this teaching is that it helps to obtain results even without substantial accumulation of merit. At a certain moment the *'dgongs pa,'* *the mind treasure* appears miraculously. By following these teachings, we can transform this body of aggregates into the Light Body, i.e. *Sambhogakaya (longs sku),* in this life itself. Having wandered for three years in the abode of 'Odmin Tugpo Kodpa, we will be praised by the holders of the system of instruction in the heaven of miracle jewels *Dharmakaya (chos sku).* Many *vidyadhara,* who themselves obtained deliverance by means of these instructions, have been constantly appearing.

It is predicted that in the future as well, by the power of the spontaneous benediction from the teachings of these supreme instructions, *tsesum (btsas gsum)* will become visible in this world.

I hope these teachings will serve as a means of completing the potentialities of the reader, since these teachings provide an intelligible and attractive means not only to understand this materialistic world but also to fully realize ourselves.

STRICKEN BY ACQUISITION, PROTECTION, AND MULTIPLICATION,
BE IT KHOWN THAT WEALTH IS AN ENDLESS SOURCE OF DISASTER.

NAGARJUNA

ABBREVIATIONS

KYTR : mkha 'gro yang thig gi gter 'byung rin po che'i lo rgyus by Klong Chen pa.

PTPT : Padma bkha'i thang Part II Tibet (in life and liberation of Padsambhava), Teshe Tshogyal.

BNKP : Autobiography of Padmalingpa

RSPL : Pad gling lo rgyus drang gtam by Padma Tshe Wang (Lopon Nado).

JGP3 : 'Jigs med ling pa pad dgu, vol. III.

KSC : mkha' 'gro'i gsang gtam chen mo by Jigmedlingpa.

NTG : gnad byang thugs kyi sgron bu by Jigmedlingpa.

TCZ : rtogz brdzod chu zla'i gar mkhan by Jigmedlingpa.

DEH : rdo grub chen 'jigs med phrin las 'od zer gi rnam mthar.

JUST AS NO SWEET SMELL IS FOUND IN A LATRINE, NO HAPPINESS IS FOUND WITHIN THE FIVE TYPES OF BEING.

LORD MAITREPA

Bibliography

I
PRIMARY SOURCES

Padmagling pa (1450-1521):rig 'dzin Padma gling pa gi zab gter chos mdzod rin po che; (the complete gter-ma discoveries of Padma gling pa)20 Vols., reprinted in Delhi 1976 at the behest of Ashi Phuntshogs Chodron.

Padma gling pa: Bumthang gter ston Padma gling Pa'i rnam thar 'od zer kun mdzes nor bu'i Phreng ba zhes bya ba skal ldan spro ba skye ba'i tshul du bris pa; (autobiography of Padma gling pa, completed by his ron rgyal ba don grub) 254 ff. in Vol. Pha of his collected works.

Padma-gling-pa?: rgyal po Sindha ra dza'i rnam thar; 30 ff. in a modern reprint, no date.

Padma gling ppa: Bum thang dar gud kyi lung bstan Padmgling pa's gter ma; (pad gling pa's gter ma prophecy on the fate of the Bum-thang provience) dbu can msin 8ff.

Kun bzang 'gyur med mchog sruh dpal 'bar (1725-1762): Kun mkhyen chos kyi rgyal po gter chen dri med 'od zer gyi rnam par thar pa cung zad spros pa ngo mtshar skal bzang mchog gi dga' ston, 33 folios, blockprint, lha lung edition. (Biography of klong chen pa dri med 'od zer, 1308-63).

Klong chen rab 'byam, dri med 'od zer (1308-63): bum thang lha's sbas yul gyi bkod pa me tog skyed tshal; ff. 22b-26b in vol. Shri of his collected works.

bdud 'joms rin po che: Gangs lgongs rgyal bstan yongs rdzogs kyi phyi mo snga 'gyur rdo rje theg pa'i bstan pa rin po che ji ltar byung ba'i tshul dag cing dsal bar brjod pa lha dbang gyul las rgyal ba'i rnga bo che'i sgra dbyangs (history of the Nyiṇgma School)Kalimpong, 1967.

O-rgyan gling pa (b.1323): bka' thang sde lnga, dga' ldan Phun tshogs gling edition of 1674.

rdzogs pa chen po klong chen Snying thig gi gdod ma'i mgon po'i lam gyi rim pa'i khrid yig ye shes bla ma (by Rang 'byung rdo rje 'jig med gling pa).

rdzogs chen yang ti nag po'i mun khrid kyi zhal shes snyan khungs brgyud pa'i man ngag zhag bdun gyis sgrub thabs.

slob dpon chen po pad ma sbyung gnas kyis mdzad pa'i man ngag lta ba'i phreng ba'i mchan 'grel nor bu'i bang mdzod (by 'Jam dbyangs blo gros rgya mtsho).

rdzogs pa chen po sems nyid rang grol (by Klong chen rab 'byams pa).

kun bzang bstan pa'i nyi ma, pad gling 'khrungs rabs kyi rt ogs brjod nyung gsal dad pa'i me tog [lives of Padmalingpa's incarnations, 1873].

slob dpon gnag mdog, 'brug rgyal khab yi chos srid gnas stangs 'b rugd kar po [general account of the history and traditions of Bhutan] (Tharpaling, 1986).

Kun mkhyen klong chen pa dri med 'od zer: mdzod bdun, (the fame seven treasuries of Vajrayana Buddhist Philosophy).

Rinpoche, Partul: Kunzang Lamahi zhyal lung, (Delhi-1983).

Kun mkhyen klong chenpa dri med 'od zer: Nal so skor gsum (Trilogy of Finding Comfort and Ease) Vols.3 (Delhi-1983).

Jigmelingpa: 'Jigs gling pa pad dgu Vol. III & VII, (Delhi-1985).

Dogrubchen Rinpoche: rdo drub chen 'jigs med phrin las 'od zer gi rnam thar (Delhi-1985).

Dudjom Rinpoche, Jigdral Yeshe Dorje (bdul 'joms 'jigs bral ye shes rdo rje). rnying m chos 'byung (gangs ljongs rgyal bstan yong rdzogs kyi phyi mo snga 'gyur rdo rje thag pa'i bstan pa rin po che'i ji ltar byung ba'i tshul dag cing gsal bar brjod pa lha dbang gyul las rgyal ba'i rnga bo che'i sgra dbyangs [History of the Nyingma school of Tibetan Buddhism]. In collected Writings and Relations of H.H. bDud-'joms rin po che 'jigs bral ye shes rdo rje, vol.1.

gter ston brgya rta'i rnam thar [The lives of the hundred treasure discovers]. In vol. 1 of the rin chen gter mdzod.

Jamyang Khyentse Wangpo. The Collected Works (gsung 'bum) of the great 'jams dbyangs mkhyen brtse'i dbang po, 13 vols. Gangtok: Gonpo Tseden 1977-80.

Khetsun Sangpo. Biographical Dictionary of Tibet and Tibetan Buddhism.14 vols. Dharamsala: Library of Tibetan Works and Archives, 1981-92 [BD].

Orgyen Lingpa (gter ston o rgyan gling pa). Padma bka' thang[The life of Guru Padmasambhava]. Chengdu: Sichuan Nationalities Press, 1987.

Ratna Lingpa, Terton. Collected Rediscovered Teachings of Ratna gling-pa 19 Vols. Darjeeling: Taklung Tsetrul Pema Wangyal, 1977-79.

II
PRIMARY SOURCES

Karmay, Samten Gyaltshan: A Discussion on the Doctrinal Position of rDzog Chen from the 10th to the 13th Cens. In Journal Asistique. Vol. 263: 147-156.

Obermiller, E. (tr.): History of Buddhism (Chos-'Byung) By Bu-ston. Heidelberg, 1932.

Roerich, G.N. (tr.): The Blue Annals (Deb-ther Sngon-Po) 2 vols. Calcutta, 1949.

Rao, S.K. Ramachandra: Tibetan Tantric Tradition, New Delhi, Arnold Heineman, 1977.

Richardson, Hugh E.: Tibet and its History, London, 1962.

Tucci, G.: The Debther Marpo Sarma: Tibetan Chronicles, (Rome, 1971).

Hoffman, H.: The Religions of Tibet, London, 1961.

Rinpoche, Kalu: The Gem Ornament of Manifold Oral

Instructions, USA, 1987.

Hopkins, Jeffrey, (tr.): Tantric Practice in Nying-ma, USA, 1986.

Rinpoche, Tulku Thondup: Buddhist Civilization in Tibet, UK, 1987.

Pande, G.C.: Studies in the Origins of Buddhism, Delhi, 1983.

Kazi Dawa-Samdrup Lama: (Tr.) The Tibetan Book of the Dead, Great Britian, 1957.

Hopkins, Jeffrey: The Tantric Distinction, London, 1984.

Hopkins, Jeffrey: Emptiness Yoga, New York, 1987.

Dutt, Nalinasha: Mahayana Buddhism, Delhi, 1978.

Lobsang Tharchen Geshe & Engle B. Artemus: Nagarjuna's Letter, (Tibetan Works & Archives, Dharamsala, 1979).

Newland, Guy: Compassion: a Tibetan Analysis, London, 1984.

Aris, Michael: Hidden Treasures and Secret Lives, Delhi, 1988.

Guenther, Harbet V. (Tr.): Jewel Ornament of Liberation by by Gampopa. Boulder, Shambhala, 1971.

Mcleond, Kenneth,: (tr.) Writings of Kalu-Rinpoche Vancouver, Kgyu Kunkhyab Chuling, 1976.

Dasgupta, S.B.: An Introduction to Tantric Buddhism, Calcutta, 1958.

Wayman, A.: Female Energy and Symbolization in the Buddhist Tantras', History of Religions, vol. 2, (1962).

Waddell, L.A.: The Buddhism of Tibet, or Lamaism, London, 1895.

Tucci, Giuseppe: The Religions of Tibet, Great Britain, 1980.

Bhutia, Dr. T.D.: Beyond Eternity Through Mysticism, Darjeeling, 1984.

Conze, E. : rNyingmapa Seet of Tibetan Buddhism, Oxford, 1951.

Sinha, Nirmal C.: An Introduction to the History and Religion of Tibet, Calcutta, 1965.

Daniel Cogort" Yoga Tantra an Introduction to Esoteric Buddhism of Tibet, New York, 1986.

Kenneth Douglas and Gwendolyn Bays: The Life and Liberation of Pdamasambhava Part-I and II Yeshe Tshogyal, USA, 1978.

Sangharakshita: A Survey of Buddhism Channel Islands, 1987.

Guenter, V. Herbert and Trungpa, Chogyam: The Dawn of Tantra.

Norbu, Tenzin: (Tr.) A Guide to Bodhisattvas Way of Life, England, 1980.

Lama Thubten Yeshe and Zopa Rinpoche: Wisdom-Energy. Honolulu: Publications for Wisdom Culture, 1976.

Geshe Sopa and Hopkins, J.: (Tr.) Practice and Theory of Tibet Buddhism. London: Rider, 1976.

Dilgo Khyentse Rinpoche. The Wish-fulfilling Jewel. The Practice of Guru Yoga according to the Longchen Nyingthig Tradition. Boston: Shambhala, 1988.

Dowman, Keith, trans. The Legend of the Great Stupa [Translation of the mchos rten chen po bya rung kha shor gi lo rgyus thos pas grol ba]. Berkeley, Calif. Dharma Publishing, 1973.

"The Stupa of Bodhnath: A Preliminary Analysis of the Written Sources." Ancient Nepal: Journal of the Department of Archeology (Kathmandu), no. 120 (Oct- Nov. 1990).

__'trans. Kindly Bent to Ease Us. by Gyalwa Longchenpa, parts1-3. Emeryville, Calif.: Dharma Publishing, 1975-1976.

Snellgrove, D.L.: The Hevajra Tantra. Pts. 1 and 2. London Orientation Series, vol. 6. London: Oxford University Press, 1961.

Thondup, Tulku Rinpoche. The Tantric Tradition of the Nyingmapa: The Origin of Buddhism in Tibet. Marion: Buddhayana Foundation, 1984.

Hidden Teachings of Tibet: An Explanation of the Terma Tradition of the Nyingma school of Buddhism. London: Wisdom, 1986.

Buddha Mind: An Anthology of Longchen Rabjams's Writings on Dzogpa Chenpo. Ithaca, N.Y.: Snow Lion, 1989.[BM].

Yeshe Tsogyal. The Lotus Born Guru. The Life Story of Padmasambhava. Revealed by Nyang Ral Nyima Ozer. Translated by Erik Padma Kunzang. Boston: Shambhala, 1993.

IF THE DHARMA IS NOT FOLLOWED AS DHARMA THE DHARMA ITSELF MAY BE THE CAUSE FOR GOING TO HELL AGAIN.

NYAM-ME DAGPO RINPOCHE

༄༅། །རྫོགས་པ་ཆེན་པོ་ཀློང་ཆེན་སྙིང་ཐིག་གི་སྔོན་འགྲོའི་ངག་
འདོན་ཁྲིགས་སུ་བསྡེབས་པ་རྣམ་མཁྱེན་ལམ་བཟང་
ཞེས་བྱ་བ་བཞུགས་སོ།།

༄༅ གདོད་ནས་མངོན་སངས་རྒྱས་ཀྱང་གང་ལ་གང་འདུལ་གཟུགས་སྐུ་འགགས་པ་མེད།
སྣ་ཚོགས་སྒྱུ་འཕྲུལ་རོལ་ཡང་ཕུང་ཁམས་སྐྱེ་མཆེད་གཟུང་དང་འཛིན་པ་བྲལ།
མི་ཡི་གཟུགས་སུ་སྣང་ཡང་མཁྱེན་བརྩེའི་འོད་ཟེར་སྟོང་འབར་རྒྱལ་བ་དངོས།
ཚེ་འདི་ཙམ་དུ་མ་ཡིན་གཏན་གྱི་སྐྱབས་སུ་ཆེད་བསྟེན་བྱིན་གྱིས་རློབས།།

དེ་ལ་འདིར་རྫོགས་པ་ཆེན་པོ་ཀློང་ཆེན་སྙིང་ཐིག་གི་ སྔོན་དུ་འགྲོ་བའི་ངག་འདོན་ཁྲིགས་སུ་
སྡེབས་པར།

དང་པོ་དཔལ་ལྡན་བླ་མའི་ཐུགས་རྒྱུད་བསྐུལ་ཕྱིར་གསོལ་བ་གདབ་པ་ནི།

༡ བླ་མ་མཁྱེན།

ཡན་གསུམ། ཞེས་གདུང་བ་དྲག་པོས་བོས་ནས།

༡ སྙིང་དབུས་དད་པའི་གེསར་བཞད་པ་ནས།
༢ སྐྱབས་གཅིག་དྲིན་ཅན་བླ་མ་ཡར་ལ་བཞེངས།
༣ ལས་དང་ཉོན་མོངས་དྲག་པོས་གཟིར་བ་ཡི།
༤ སྐལ་བ་ངན་པ་བདག་ལ་སྐྱོབ་པའི་ཕྱིར།
༥ སྤྱི་བོ་བདེ་ཆེན་འཁོར་ལོའི་རྒྱན་དུ་བཞུགས།
༦ དྲན་དང་ཤེས་བཞིན་ཀུན་ཀྱང་བཞེངས་སུ་གསོལ།

༡ ད་རེས་དམྱལ་བ་ཡི་དྭགས་དུད་འགྲོ་དང་།
༢ ཚེ་རིང་ལྷ་དང་ཀླ་ཀློ་ལོག་ལྟ་ཅན།
༣ སངས་རྒྱས་མ་བྱོན་ཞིང་དང་ལྐུགས་པ་སྐྱེ།
༤ མི་ཁོམ་བརྒྱད་ལས་ཐར་བའི་དལ་བ་ཐོབ།

༥ མིར་གྱུར་དབང་པོ་ཚང་དང་ཡུལ་དབུས་སྐྱེས།

༦ ལས་མཐའ་མ་ལོག་བསྟན་ལ་དད་པ་སྟེ།

༧ རང་ཉིད་འབྱོར་བ་ལྔ་ཚང་སངས་རྒྱས་བྱོན།

༨ ཆོས་གསུངས་བསྟན་པ་གནས་དང་དེ་ལ་ཞུགས།

༩ བཤེས་གཉེན་དམ་པས་ཟིན་དང་གཞན་འབྱོར་ལྔ།

༡༠ ཐམས་ཅད་རང་ལ་ཚང་བའི་གནས་ཐོབ་ཀྱང་།

༡༡ རྐྱེན་མང་ངེས་པ་མེད་པའི་ཆོས་སྤངས་ནས།

༡༢ འཇིག་རྟེན་ཕ་རོལ་ཉིད་དུ་སོན་པར་འགྱུར།

༡༣ བློ་སྣ་ཆོས་ལ་བསྒྱུར་ཅིག་གུ་རུ་མཁྱེན།

༡༤ ལམ་ལོག་དམན་པར་མ་གཏོང་ཀུན་མཁྱེན་རྗེ།

༡༥ གཉིས་སུ་མེད་དོར་རྡོ་རྗེ་ཅན་བླ་མ་མཁྱེན།

༡ ད་རེས་དལ་རྟེན་དོན་ཡོད་མ་བྱས་ན།

༢ ཕྱིས་ནས་ཐར་པ་བསྒྲུབ་པའི་རྟེན་མི་རྙེད།

༣ བདེ་འགྲོའི་རྟེན་ལ་བསོད་ནམས་ཟད་གྱུར་ནས།

༤ ཤི་བའི་རོག་ཏུ་ངན་སོང་ངན་འགྲོར་འཁྱམས།

༥ དགེ་སྡིག་མི་ཤེས་ཆོས་ཀྱི་སྒྲ་མི་ཐོས།

༦ དགེ་བའི་བཤེས་དང་མི་མཇལ་མཚང་རེ་ཆེ།

༧ སེམས་ཅན་ཙམ་གྱི་གྲངས་དང་རིམ་པ་ལ།

༨ བསམས་ན་མི་ལུས་ཐོབ་པ་སྲིད་མཐའ་ཙམ།

༩ མི་ཡང་ཆོས་མེད་སྡིག་ལ་སྤྱོད་མཐོང་ན།

༡༠ ཆོས་བཞིན་སྤྱོད་པ་ཉིན་མོའི་སྐར་མ་ཙམ།

༡༡ བློ་སྣ་ཆོས་ལ་བསྒྱུར་ཅིག་གུ་རུ་མཁྱེན།

༡༢ ལམ་གོལ་དམན་པར་མ་གཏོང་ཀུན་མཁྱེན་ཧཻ།

༡༣ གཉིས་སུ་མེད་དོ་དྲིན་ཅན་བླ་མ་མཁྱེན།

༡ ག་ལ་ཏེ་མི་ལུས་རིན་ཆེན་གླིང་ཕྱིན་ཡང་།

༢ ལུས་རྟེན་བཟང་ལ་བྱུར་པོ་ཆེ་ཡི་སེམས།

༣ ཐར་པ་བསྒྲུབ་པའི་རྟེན་དུ་མི་རུང་ཞིང་།

༤ ཁྱད་པར་བདུད་ཀྱིས་ཟིན་དང་དུག་ལྔ་འཁྲུགས།

༥ ལས་ངན་ཐོག་ཏུ་བབས་དང་ལེ་ལོས་གཡེངས།

༦ གཞན་ཁོལ་བྲན་གཡོག་འཇིགས་སྐྱོབ་ཆོས་ལྟར་བཅོས།

༧ རྨོངས་སོགས་པ་འཕྲུལ་བྱུང་རྐྱེན་གྱི་མི་ཁོམ་བརྒྱད།

༨ བདག་ལ་ཆོས་ཀྱི་འགལ་ལ་ཟླར་ལྷགས་པའི་ཚེ།

༩ བློ་སྣ་ཆོས་ལ་བསྒྱུར་ཅིག་གུ་རུ་མཁྱེན།

༡༠ ལམ་གོལ་དམན་པར་མ་གཏོང་ཀུན་མཁྱེན་ཧཻ།

༡༡ གཉིས་སུ་མེད་དོ་དྲིན་ཅན་བླ་མ་མཁྱེན།

༡ སྐྱེ་ཤས་ཆུང་ཞིང་དད་པའི་ནོར་དང་བྲལ།

༢ འདོད་སྲེད་ཞགས་པས་བཅིངས་དང་ཀུན་སྤྱོད་རྒྱུ།

༣ མི་དགེ་སྡིག་ལ་མི་འཛེམ་ལས་མཐའ་ལོག

༤ སྡོམ་པ་ཉམས་ཤིང་དམ་ཚིག་རལ་བ་སྐྱེ།

༥ རིས་ཆད་གློ་ཡི་མི་ཁྱིམ་རྣམ་པ་བརྒྱུད།

༦ བདག་ལ་ཆོས་ཀྱི་འགལ་ཟླར་ལྷགས་པའི་ཚེ།

༧ བློ་ཁ་ཆོས་ལ་བསྒྱུར་ཅིག་གུ་རུ་མཁྱེན།

༨ ལམ་གོལ་དམན་པར་མ་གཏོང་ཀུན་མཁྱེན་རྗེ།

༩ གཉིས་སུ་མེད་དོ་དྲིན་ཅན་བླ་མ་མཁྱེན།

༡ ད་ལྟ་ནད་དང་སྡུག་བསྔལ་གྱིས་མ་ག་ཟེར།

༢ ཐན་ཁོལ་ལ་སོགས་གཞན་དབང་མ་གྱུར་པས།

༣ རང་དབང་ཐོབ་པའི་རྟེན་འབྲེལ་འགྲིག་དུས་འདིར།

༤ སྨོམས་ལས་ངང་དུ་དལ་འབྱོར་རྒྱུད་གསོན་ན།

༥ འཁོར་དང་ལོངས་སྤྱོད་ཉེ་དུ་འབྲེལ་བ་ལྟ།

༦ ལྟ་ཅི་གཅེས་པར་བཟུང་བའི་ལུས་འདི་ཡང་།

༧ མལ་གྱི་ནང་ནས་ས་ཕྱོགས་སྟོང་པར་བསྐྱལ།

༨ ཝ་དང་ཁྲ་རྒོད་ཁྱི་ཡིས་འདྲུད་པའི་དུས།

༩ བར་དོའི་ཡུལ་ན་འཇིགས་པ་ཤིན་ཏུ་ཆེ།

༡༠ བློ་ཁ་ཆོས་ལ་བསྒྱུར་ཅིག་གུ་རུ་མཁྱེན།

༡༡ ལམ་གོལ་དམན་པར་མ་གཏོང་ཀུན་མཁྱེན་རྗེ།

༡༢ གཉིས་སུ་མེད་དོ་དྲིན་ཅན་བླ་མ་མཁྱེན།

༡ དགེ་སྡིག་ལས་ཀྱི་རྣམ་སྨིན་ཕྱི་བཞིན་འབྲང་།

༡ ཁྱད་པར་དམྱལ་བའི་འཇིག་རྟེན་ཉིད་སྔོན་ནས།

༢ ལྕགས་བསྲེགས་གཞིར་མཚོན་གྱིས་མགོ་ལུས་འདྲལ།

༣ སོག་ལེས་གཤོག་དང་ཐོ་ལུམ་འབར་བས་འཚིར།

༤ སྒོ་མེད་ལྕགས་ཁྱིམ་འཁྱུམས་པར་འོ་དོད་འབོད།

༥ འབར་བའི་གསལ་ཤིང་གིས་འབུགས་གྲོ་ཀུར་འཚོད།

༦ ཀུན་ནས་ཚ་བའི་མེས་བསྲེགས་བརྒྱད་ཚན་གཅིག

༧ གངས་རི་སྟུག་པོའི་འདབ་བྲ་དང་ཆུ་འཁྱགས་ཀྱི།

༨ གཅོང་རོང་ཡ་ངའི་གནས་སུ་བུ་ཡུག་སྦྲེབས།

༩ གྲང་རེག་ཀླུང་གིས་བཏབ་པའི་ཡང་ཚོ་ནི།

༡༠ ཆུ་བུར་ཅན་དང་ལྷག་པར་བརྡོལ་བ་ཅན།

༡༡ སྨྲེ་སྔགས་རྒྱུན་མི་ཆད་པར་འདོན་པ་ཡང་།

༡༢ ཚེར་བའི་སྡུག་བསྔལ་བརྟག་པར་དཀའ་བ་ཡིས།

༡༣ ཀྱུངས་ཀྱིས་རབ་བཏང་འཚི་ཁའི་ནད་པ་བཞིན།

༡༤ ཤུགས་རིང་འདོན་ཅིང་སོ་ཐམ་པགས་པ་འགས།

༡༥ ཤའུ་ཐོན་ནས་ལྷག་པར་འགས་ཏེ་བརྒྱད།

༡༦ དེ་བཞིན་སྐྱུ་གྲིའི་ཐང་ལ་རྐང་པ་གཤོགས།

༡༧ རལ་གྲིའི་ཚལ་དུ་ལུས་ལ་བཅད་གཏུབས་བྱེད།

༡༨ རོ་མྱགས་འདམ་རྫུད་···ཐལ་ཚན་རབ་མེད་ཀློང་།

༡༩ མནར་བའི་ཉེ་འཁོར་བ་དང་འགྱུར་བ་ཅན།

༢༠ སྨོ་དང་ཀ་བ་ཐབ་དང་ཐག་པ་སོགས།

༢༡ རྟག་ཏུ་བཀོལ་ཞིང་སྤྱོད་པའི་ཉེ་ཚེ་བ།

༢༢ ནམ་གྲངས་བཅོ་བརྒྱད་གང་ལས་འབྱུང་བའི་རྒྱུ།

༢༣ ཞེ་སྡང་དྲག་པོའི་ཀུན་སློང་སྐྱེས་པའི་ཚེ།

༢༤ བློ་སྣ་ཆོས་ལ་བསྒྱུར་ཅིག་གུ་རུ་མཁྱེན།

༢༥ ལམ་གོལ་དམན་པར་མ་གཏོང་ཀུན་མཁྱེན་རྗེ།

༢༦ གཉིས་སུ་མེད་དོ་དྲིན་ཅན་བླ་མ་མཁྱེན།

༡ དེ་བཞིན་ཡོངས་ལ་ཉམས་མི་དགའ་བའི་ཡུལ།

༢ བཟའ་བཏུང་ལོངས་སྤྱོད་མིང་ཡང་མི་གྲགས་པར།

༣ ཟས་སྐོམ་ལོ་བླར་མི་རྙེད་ཡི་དྭགས་ལུས།

༤ རིད་ཅིང་ལྡང་པའི་སྟོབས་ཉམས་རྣམ་པ་གསུམ།

༥ གང་ལས་འབྱུང་བའི་རྒྱུ་ནི་སེར་སྣ་ཡིན།

༦ གཅིག་ལ་གཅིག་ཟ་གསོད་པའི་འཇིགས་པ་ཆེ།

༧ བཀོལ་ཞིང་སྤྱོད་པས་ཉམ་ཐག་སྡང་དོ་རྨོངས།

༨ ཕ་མཐའ་མེད་པའི་སྡུག་བསྔལ་གྱིས་གཟིར་བའི།

༩ ས་བོན་གཏི་མུག་སྤུན་པར་འཇོམས་པ་བདག

༡༠ བློ་སྣ་ཆོས་ལ་བསྒྱུར་ཅིག་གུ་རུ་མཁྱེན།

༡༡ ལམ་གོལ་དམན་པར་མ་གཏོང་ཀུན་མཁྱེན་རྗེ།

༡༢ གཉིས་སུ་མེད་དོ་དྲིན་ཅན་བླ་མ་མཁྱེན།

༡ ཆོས་ལམ་ཞུགས་ཀྱང་ཉེས་སྤྱོད་མི་སྡོམ་ཞིང་།

༢ ཐེག་ཆེན་སྒོར་ཞུགས་གཞན་ཕན་སེམས་དང་བྲལ།

༣ དབང་བཞི་ཐོབ་ཀྱང་བསྐྱེད་རྫོགས་མི་སྒོམ་པའི།

༤ ལམ་གོལ་འདི་ལས་བླ་མས་བསྒྲལ་དུ་གསོལ།

༥ ལྟ་བ་མ་རྟོགས་ཐོ་ཅོའི་སྤྱོད་པ་ཅན།

༦ སྒོམ་པ་ཡེངས་ཀྱང་གོ་ཡུལ་འདུ་གོག་འཐག

༧ སྤྱོད་པ་ནོར་ཀྱང་རང་སྐྱོན་མི་སེམས་པའི།

༨ ཆོས་དྲེད་འདི་ལས་བླ་མས་བསྒྲལ་དུ་གསོལ།

༩ ནངས་པར་འཆི་ཡང་གནས་གོས་ནོར་ལ་སྲེད།

༡༠ ན་ཚོད་ཡོལ་ཡང་ངེས་འབྱུང་སྐྱོ་ཤས་བྲལ།

༡༡ ཐོས་པ་ཆུང་ཡང་ཡོན་ཏན་ཅན་དུ་རློམ།

༡༢ མ་རིག་འདི་ལས་བླ་མས་བསྒྲལ་དུ་གསོལ།

༡༣ རྐྱེན་ཁར་འཚོར་ཡང་འདུ་འཛི་གནས་སྐོར་སེམས།

༡༤ དབེན་པར་བརྟེན་ཀྱང་རང་··རྒྱུད་ཤིང་ལྟར་རེངས།

༡༥ དུལ་བར་སྨྲ་ཡང་ཆགས་སྡང་མ་ཞིག་པའི།

༡༦ ཆོས་བརྒྱད་འདི་ལས་བླ་མས་བསྒྲལ་དུ་གསོལ།

༡༧ གཉིད་འཐུག་འདི་ལས་མྱུར་དུ་སད་དུ་གསོལ།

༡༨ ཁྲོཾ་སྨུན་འདི་ལས་མྱུར་དུ་དབྱུང་དུ་གསོལ།།

ཞེས་འབོད་པ་དྲག་པོས་ཐུགས་རྗེ་སློངས་བར་བྱའོ།།

གཉིས་པ་སྐྱབས་སུ་འགྲོ་བ་ནི།

༡ དཀོན་མཆོག་གསུམ་དངོས་བདེ་གཤེགས་རྩ་བ་གསུམ༔
༢ རྩ་རླུང་ཐིག་ལེའི་རང་བཞིན་བྱང་ཆུབ་སེམས༔
༣ ངོ་བོ་རང་བཞིན་ཐུགས་རྗེའི་དཀྱིལ་འཁོར་ལ༔
༤ བྱང་ཆུབ་སྙིང་པོའི་བར་དུ་སྐྱབས་སུ་མཆི༔

ལན་གསུམ༔

གསུམ་པ་སེམས་བསྐྱེད་ནི།

༡ ཧོ༔ སྣ་ཚོགས་སྣང་བ་ཆུ་ཟླའི་རྫུན་རིས་ཀྱིས༔
༢ འཁོར་བ་ལུ་གུ་རྒྱུད་དུ་འཁྱམས་པའི་འགྲོ༔
༣ རང་རིག་འོད་གསལ་དབྱིངས་སུ་ངལ་གསོའི་ཕྱིར༔
༤ ཚད་མེད་བཞི་ཡི་ངང་ནས་སེམས་བསྐྱེད་དོ༔

ལན་གསུམ༔

བཞི་པ་རྡོར་སེམས་བསྒོམ་བཟླས་ནི།

༡ ཨཱཿ བདག་ཉིད་ཐམ་ལ་སྤྱི་བོ་རུ༔
༢ པད་དཀར་ཟླ་བའི་གདན་གྱི་དབུས༔
༣ ཧཱུྃ་ལས་བླ་མ་རྡོ་རྗེ་སེམས༔
༤ དཀར་གསལ་ལོངས་སྤྱོད་རྫོགས་པའི་སྐུ༔

༥ རྡོ་རྗེ་དྲིལ་འཛིན་སྙེམས་མ་འཁྲིལ༔

༦ ཁྱོད་ལ་སྐྱབས་གསོལ་སྡིག་པ་སྦྱོང༔

༧ འགྱོད་སེམས་དྲག་པོས་མཐོལ་ལོ་བཤགས༔

༨ ཕྱིན་ཆད་སྲོག་ལ་བབ་ཀྱང་སྡོམ༔

༩ ཁྱོད་ཐུགས་ཟླ་བ་རྒྱས་པའི་སྟེང༔

༡༠ ཧཱུྃ་ཡིག་མཐའ་མར་སྔགས་ཀྱིས་བསྐོར༔

༡༡ བཟླས་པ་སྔགས་ཀྱིས་རྒྱུད་བསྐུལ་བས༔

༡༢ ཡབ་ཡུམ་བདེ་རོལ་སྦྱོར་མཚམས་ནས༔

༡༣ བདུད་རྩི་བྱང་ཆུབ་སེམས་ཀྱི་སྤྲིན༔

༡༤ གབུར་རྡུལ་ལྟར་འཛགས་པ་ཡིས༔

༡༥ བདག་དང་ཁམས་གསུམ་སེམས་ཅན་གྱི༔

༡༦ ལས་དང་ཉོན་མོངས་སྡུག་བསྔལ་རྒྱུ༔

༡༧ ནད་གདོན་སྡིག་སྒྲིབ་ཉེས་ལྟུང་གྲིབ༔

༡༨ མ་ལུས་བྱང་བར་མཛད་དུ་གསོལ༔

༡ ཨོཾ་བཛྲ་ས་ཏྭ་ས་མ་ཡ༔

༢ མ་ནུ་པཱ་ལ་ཡ༔

༣ བཛྲ་ས་ཏྭ་ཏེ་ནོ་པ༔

༤ ཏིཥྛ་དྲྀ་ཌྷོ་མེ་བྷ་ཝ༔

༥ སུ་ཏོ་ཥྱོ་མེ་བྷ་ཝ༔

༦ སུ་པོ་ཥྱོ་མེ་བྷ་ཝ༔

༧ ཨ་ནུ་ར་ཀྟོ་མེ་བྷ་ཝ༔

༨ སརྦ་སིདྡྷི་མྨེ་པྲ་ཡཙྪ༔

༩ སརྦ་ཀརྨ་སུ་ཙ་མེ༔

༡༠ ཙིཏྟཾ་ཤྲེ་ཡཿ་ཀུ་རུ་ཧཱུྃ༔

༡༡ ཧ་ཧ་ཧ་ཧ་ཧོ༔

༡༢ བྷ་ག་ཝཱན་སརྦ་ཏ་ཐཱ་ག་ཏ་བཛྲ་མཱ་མེ་མུཉྩ༔

༡༣ བཛྲི་བྷ་ཝ་མ་ཧཱ་ས་མ་ཡ་སཏྭ་ཨཱ༔

ཞེས་ཡི་གེ་བརྒྱ་པ་ཅི་ནུས་བཟླས་མཐར།

༡ མགོན་པོ་བདག་ནི་མི་ཤེས་རྨོངས་པ་ཡིས༔

༢ དམ་ཚིག་ལས་ནི་འགལ་ཞིང་ཉམས༔

༣ བླ་མ་མགོན་པོས་སྐྱབས་མཛོད་ཅིག༔

༤ གཙོ་བོ་རྡོ་རྗེ་འཛིན་པ་སྟེ།

༥ ཐུགས་རྗེ་ཆེན་པོའི་བདག་ཉིད་ཅན༔

༦ འགྲོ་བའི་གཙོ་ལ་བདག་སྐྱབས་མཆི༔

༡ སྐུ་གསུང་ཐུགས་རྩ་བ་དང་ཡན་ལག་གི་དམ་ཚིག་ཉམས་པ་ཐམས་ཅད་མཐོལ་ལོ་བཤགས་སོ༔

༢ སྡིག་པ་དང་སྒྲིབ་པ་ཉེས་ལྟུང་དྲི་མའི་ཚོགས་ཐམས་ཅད་བྱང་ཞིང་དག་པར་མཛད་དུ་གསོལ༔

༣ ཅེས་བརྗོད་པས་རྡོ་རྗེ་སེམས་དཔའ་དགྱེས་བཞིན་འཛུམ་པ་དང་བཅས་
པས་རིགས་ཀྱི་བུ་ཁྱོད་ཀྱི་སྡིག་སྒྲིབ་ཉེས་ལྟུང་ཐམས་ཅད་དག་པ་ཡིན་ནོ།
ཞེས་གནང་བ་བྱིན་ཞིང་། འོད་དུ་ཞུ་ནས་ རང་ལ་ཐིམ་པའི་རྐྱེན་ལས།
༤ རང་ཉིད་ཀྱང་... རྡོ་རྗེ་སེམས་དཔའ་... སྣང་སྟོང་མེ་ལོང་ནང་གི་གཟུགས་བརྙན་
ལྟ་བུར་གྱུར་པའི་ ཐུགས་སྲོག་ཧཱུྃ་གི་མཐའ་མར་ ཡི་གེར་འབྲུ་བཞི་པོ་...
གསལ་བ་ལས་... འོད་ཟེར་འཕྲོས་ ཁམས་གསུམ་སྣོད་བཅུད་དང་བཅས་པ་
རྡོར་སེམས་པ་རིགས་ལྔའི་རྟེན་དང་བརྟེན་པའི་རང་བཞིན་དུ་ སངས་རྒྱས་པར་
བསམས་ལ།

༥ ཨོཾ་བཛྲ་སཏྭ་ཧཱུྃ༔

ཅེས་བཟླས་མཐར་མཉམ་པར་བཞག་གོ།

ཞུ་པ་མཎྜ་ལ་ནི།

༡ ཨོཾ་ཨཱཿཧཱུྃ། སྟོང་གསུམ་འཇིག་རྟེན་བྱེ་བ་ཕྲག་བརྒྱའི་ཞིང་༔
༢ རིན་ཆེན་སྣ་བདུན་ལྷ་མིའི་འབྱོར་པས་གཏམས༔
༣ བདག་ལུས་ལོངས་སྤྱོད་བཅས་པ་ཡོངས་འབུལ་གྱིས༔
༤ ཆོས་ཀྱི་འཁོར་ལོས་སྒྱུར་བའི་སྲིད་ཐོབ་ཤོག༔
༡ འོག་མིན་བདེ་ཆེན་སྟུག་པོ་བཀོད་པའི་ཞིང་༔
༢ ངེས་པ་ལྔ་ལྡན་རིགས་ལྔའི་ཚོམ་བུ་ཅན༔
༣ འདོད་ཡོན་མཆོད་པའི་སྤྲིན་ཕུང་བསམ་ཡས་པ༔
༤ ཕུལ་བས་ལོངས་སྐུའི་ཞིང་ལ་སྤྱོད་པར་ཤོག༔

༡ སྣང་སྲིད་རྣམ་དག་གཞོན་ནུ་བུམ་པའི་སྐུ༔

༢ ཐུགས་རྗེ་མ་འགགས་ཆོས་ཉིད་རོལ་པས་བརྒྱན༔

༣ སྐུ་དང་ཐིག་ལེའི་འཛིན་པ་རྣམ་དག་ཞིང༔

༤ ཐུལ་བས་ཆོས་སྐུའི་ཞིང་ལ་སྤྱོད་པར་ཤོག༔

ཐུག་པ་ཀུ་སུ་ལུའི་ཚོགས་གསོག་གཞི༔

༡ ཕཊ༔ ལུས་གཅེས་འཛིན་བོར་བས་ལྷ་བདུད་ཆོམ༔

༢ སེམས་ཚངས་པའི་སྒོ་ནས་དབྱིངས་ལ་ཐོན༔

༣ འཆི་བདག་གི་བདུད་བཅོམ་ཁྲོས་མར་གྱུར༔

༤ གཡས་ཉོན་མོངས་བདུད་འཇོམས་ཀྱི་གྲི་གུག་གིས༔

༥ གཟུགས་ཕུང་པོའི་བདུད་བཅོམ་ཐོད་པ་བྲེགས༔

༦ གཡོན་ལས་བྱེད་རྐྱལ་གྱིས་ཐྭ་ཐྲྭ་ཐོགས༔

༧ སྐུ་གསུམ་གྱི་མི་མགོའི་སྒྲེད་པུར་བཞག༔

༨ ནང་སྟོང་གསུམ་གང་བའི་བམ་རོ་དེ༔

༩ ཨཱཿཐུང་དང་ཧཾ་ཡིག་གིས་བདུད་རྩིར་བཞུ༔

༡༠ འབྲུ་གསུམ་གྱི་ནུས་པས་སྦྱང་སྤེལ་བསྒྱུར༔

༡ ཨོཾ་ཨཱཿཧཱུྃ། ཚིག་བསྡུས་མཐར་

༡ ཕཊ༔ ཡར་མཆོད་ཡུལ་མགྲོན་གྱི་ཐུགས་དམ་བསྐང༔

༢ ཚོགས་རྫོགས་ནས་མཆོག་ཐུན་དངོས་གྲུབ་ཐོབ༔

༣ མར་འཁོར་བའི་མགྲོན་མ་ཉེས་ལན་ཆགས་བྱང༔

༤ ཁྱད་པར་གནོད་བྱེད་བགེགས་རིགས་ཚོམ༔

༥ ནད་གདོན་དང་བར་ཆད་དབྱིངས་སུ་ཞི༔

༦ རྒྱེན་ངན་དང་བདག་འཛིན་རྡུལ་དུ་བརླགས༔

༧ མཐར་མཆོད་བྱ་དང་མཆོད་བྱེད་མཆོད་ཡུལ་ཀུན༔

༨ གཉིས་རྫོགས་པ་ཆེན་པོར་མ་བཅོས་ཨཱ༔

བདུན་པ་བླ་མའི་རྣལ་འབྱོར་ནི།

༡ ཨེ་མ་ཧོ༔ རང་སྣང་ལྷུན་གྲུབ་དག་པ་རབ་འབྱམས་ཞིང༔

༢ བཀོད་པ་རབ་རྫོགས་ཟངས་མདོག་དཔལ་རིའི་དབུས༔

༣ རང་ཉིད་གཞི་ལུས་རྡོ་རྗེ་རྣལ་འབྱོར་མ༔

༤ ཞལ་གཅིག་ཕྱག་གཉིས་དམར་གསལ་གྲི་ཐོད་འཛིན༔

༥ ཞབས་གཉིས་དོར་སྟབས་སྤྱན་གསུམ་ནམ་མཁར་གཟིགས༔

༦ སྤྱི་བོར་པདྨ་འབུམ་བརྡལ་ཉི་ཟླའི་སྟེང༔

༧ སྐྱབས་གནས་ཀུན་འདུས་རྩ་བའི་བླ་མ་དང༔

༨ དབྱེར་མེད་མཚོ་སྐྱེས་རྡོ་རྗེ་སྤྲུལ་པའི་སྐུ༔

༩ དཀར་དམར་མདངས་ལྡན་གཞོན་ནུའི་ཉ་ཚུགས་ཅན༔

༡༠ ཕོད་ཀ་ཆོས་གོས་ཟ་བེར་འཛུང་མ་གསོལ༔

༡༡ ཞལ་གཅིག་ཕྱག་གཉིས་རྒྱལ་པོའི་རོལ་པའི་སྟབས༔

༡༢ ཕྱག་གཡས་རྡོ་རྗེ་གཡོན་པས་ཐོད་ཁྲུམ་བསྣམས༔

༡༣ དགྱེས་འདབ་ལྡན་པདྨའི་མཉེན་ཞུ་གསོལ༔

༡༤ མཆན་ཁུང་གཡོན་ན་བདེ་སྟོང་ཡུམ་མཆོག་སྨ༔

༡༥ སྦས་པའི་ཚུལ་གྱིས་ཁ་ཊྭཾ་རྩེ་གསུམ་བསྣམས༔

༡༦ འཇའ་ཟེར་ཐིག་ལེའི་འོད་ཕུང་ཀློང་ན་བཞུགས༔

༡༧ ཕྱི་འཁོར་འོད་ལྔའི་དྲྭ་བས་མཛེས་པའི་ཀློང༔

༡༨ སྤྲུལ་པའི་རྗེ་འབངས་ཉི་ཤུ་རྩ་ལྔ་དང༔

༡༩ རྒྱ་བོད་པཎ་གྲུབ་རིག་འཛིན་ཡི་དམ་ལྷ༔

༢༠ མཁའ་འགྲོ་ཆོས་སྐྱོང་དམ་ཅན་སྤྲིན་ལྟར་གཏིབས༔

༢༡ གསལ་སྟོང་མཉམ་གནས་ཆེན་པོའི་ངང་དུ་གསལ༔

༡ ཧཱུྃ། ཨོ་རྒྱན་ཡུལ་གྱི་ནུབ་བྱང་མཚམས༔

༢ པདྨ་གེ་སར་སྡོང་པོ་ལ༔

༣ ཡ་མཚན་མཆོག་གི་དངོས་གྲུབ་བརྙེས༔

༤ པདྨ་འབྱུང་གནས་ཞེས་སུ་གྲགས༔

༥ འཁོར་དུ་མཁའ་འགྲོ་མང་པོས་བསྐོར༔

༦ ཁྱེད་ཀྱི་རྗེས་སུ་བདག་བསྒྲུབ་ཀྱིས༔

༧ བྱིན་གྱིས་བརླབ་ཕྱིར་གཤེགས་སུ་གསོལ༔

༨ གུ་རུ་པདྨ་སིདྡྷི་ཧཱུྃ༔

༡ ཧཱུྃ༔ བདག་ལུས་ཞིང་གི་རྡུལ་སྙེད་དུ༔
༢ རྣམ་པར་འཕྲུལ་པས་ཕྱག་འཚལ་ལོ༔
༣ དངོས་བཤམས་ཡིད་སྤྲུལ་ཏིང་འཛིན་མཐུས༔
༤ སྣང་སྲིད་མཆོད་པའི་ཕྱག་རྒྱར་འབུལ༔
༥ སྒོ་གསུམ་མི་དགེའི་ལས་རྣམས་ཀུན༔
༦ འོད་གསལ་ཆོས་སྐུའི་ངང་དུ་བཤགས༔
༧ བདེན་པ་གཉིས་ཀྱིས་བསྡུས་པ་ཡི༔
༨ དགེ་ཚོགས་ཀུན་ལ་རྗེས་ཡི་རང༔
༩ ཐེག་གསུམ་ཆོས་འཁོར་བསྐོར་བར་བསྐུལ༔
༡༠ ཇི་སྲིད་འཁོར་བམ་སྟོངས་བར༔
༡༡ མྱ་ངན་མི་འདའ་བཞུགས་གསོལ་འདེབས༔
༡༢ དུས་གསུམ་བསགས་པའི་དགེ་རྩ་ཀུན༔
༡༣ བྱང་ཆུབ་ཆེན་པོའི་རྒྱུ་རུ་བསྔོ༔

༡ རྗེ་བཙུན་གུ་རུ་རིན་པོ་ཆེ༔
༢ ཁྱེད་ནི་སངས་རྒྱས་ཐམས་ཅད་ཀྱི༔
༣ ཐུགས་རྗེ་བྱིན་རླབས་འདུས་པའི་དཔལ༔
༤ སེམས་ཅན་ཡོངས་ཀྱི་མགོན་གཅིག་པུ༔
༥ ལུས་དང་ལོངས་སྤྱོད་བློ་སྙིང་བྲང༔
༦ ལྟོས་པ་མེད་པར་ཁྱེད་ལ་འབུལ༔

༧ འདི་ནས་བྱང་ཆུབ་མ་ཐོབ་བར༔
༨ སྐྱིད་སྡུག་ལེགས་ཉེས་མཐོ་དམན་ཀུན༔
༩ རྗེ་བཙུན་ཆེན་པོ་པད་འབྱུང་མཁྱེན༔

༡ བདག་ལ་རེ་ས་གཞན་ན་མེད༔
༢ ད་ལྟའི་དུས་ངན་སྙིགས་མའི་འགྲོ༔
༣ མི་བཟོད་སྡུག་བསྔལ་འདམ་དུ་བྱིངས༔
༤ འདི་ལས་སྐྱོབས་ཤིག་མ་ཧཱ་གུ་རུ༔
༥ དབང་བཞི་བསྐུར་ཅིག་བྱིན་རླབས་ཅན༔
༦ རྟོགས་པ་སྤྲོར་ཅིག་ཐུགས་རྗེ་ཅན༔
༧ སྒྲིབ་གཉིས་སྦྱོངས་ཤིག་ནུས་མཐུ་ཅན༔

༡ ནམ་ཞིག་ཚེ་ཡི་དུས་བྱས་ཚེ༔
༢ རང་སྣང་ཟ་ཡབ་དཔལ་རིའི་ཞིང༔
༣ ཟུང་འཇུག་སྤྲུལ་པའི་ཞིང་ཁམས་སུ༔
༤ གཞི་ལུས་རྡོ་རྗེ་རྣལ་འབྱོར་མ༔
༥ གསལ་འཚེར་འོད་ཀྱི་སྒོང་བུ་རུ༔
༦ གྱུར་ནས་རྗེ་བཙུན་པད་འབྱུང་དང༔
༧ དབྱེར་མེད་ཆེན་པོར་སངས་རྒྱས་ཏེ༔
༨ བདེ་དང་སྟོང་པའི་ཆོ་འཕྲུལ་གྱིས༔

༩ ཡེ་ཤེས་ཆེན་པོའི་རོལ་པ་ལས༔

༡༠ ཁམས་གསུམ་སེམས་ཅན་མ་ལུས་པ༔

༡༡ འདྲེན་པའི་དེད་དཔོན་དམ་པ་རྫུ༔

༡༢ རྗེ་བཙུན་པདྨས་དབུགས་དབྱུང་གསོལ༔

༡༣ གསོལ་བ་སྙིང་གི་དཀྱིལ་ནས་འདེབས༔

༡༤ ཁ་ཙམ་ཚིག་ཙམ་མ་ཡིན་ནོ༔

༡༥ བྱིན་རླབས་ཐུགས་ཀྱི་ཀློང་ནས་སྩོལ༔

༡༦ བསམ་དོན་འགྲུབ་པར་མཛད་དུ་གསོལ༔

༡ ཨོཾ་ཨཱཿཧཱུྃ་བཛྲ་གུ་རུ་པདྨ་སིདྡྷི་ཧཱུྃ༔

བརྒྱད་པ་བརྒྱུད་པའི་གསོལ་འདེབས་ནི།

༡ ཨེ་མ་ཧོ༔ རྒྱ་ཆད་ཕྱོགས་ལྷུང་བྲལ་བའི་ཞིང་ཁམས་ནས༔

༢ དང་པོའི་སངས་རྒྱས་ཆོས་སྐུ་ཀུན་ཏུ་བཟང༔

༣ ལོངས་སྐུ་ཆུ་ཟླའི་རོལ་རྩལ་རྡོ་རྗེ་སེམས་ཀས༔

༤ སྤྲུལ་སྐུར་མཚན་རྫོགས་དགའ་རབ་རྡོ་རྗེ་ལ༔

༥ གསོལ་བ་འདེབས་སོ་བྱིན་རླབས་དབང་བསྐུར་སྩོལ༔

༡ ཤྲཱི་སིངྷ་དོན་དམ་ཆོས་ཀྱི་མཛོད༔

༢ འཇམ་དཔལ་བཤེས་གཉེན་ཐེག་དགུའི་འཁོར་ལོས་བསྒྱུར༔

༣ རྡོ་ན་སུ་ཏྲ་པཏ་ཆེན་ཐིམ་ལར༔

༤ གསོལ་འདེབས་སོ་གྲོལ་བྱེད་ལམ་སྣ་སྟོན༔

༡ འཛམ་བུ་གླིང་གི་རྒྱན་གཅིག་པདྨ་འབྱུང༔

༢ ངེས་པར་ཐུགས་ཀྱི་སྲས་མཆོག་རྗེ་འབངས་གྲོགས༔

༣ ཐུགས་གཏེར་རྒྱ་མཚོའི་བདག་གྲོལ་གླིང་ཆེན་ཞབས༔

༤ མཁའ་འགྲོའི་དབྱིངས་མཛོད་བཀའ་བབས་འཇིགས་མེད་གླིང༔

༥ གསོལ་བ་འདེབས་སོ་འབྲས་བུ་ཐོབ་གྲོལ་སྩོལ༔

བརྒྱུད་འདེབས་ཁ་སྐོང་།

༡ མཁས་ཤིང་གྲུབ་བརྙེས་ཀུན་བཟང་གཞན་ཕན་དཔལ།

༢ ཕྱག་ན་པདྨོ་རྒྱལ་བའི་སྨྲ་སྒྲ་དང་།

༣ འཇམ་པའི་དབྱངས་དངོས་མཁན་ཆེན་པདྨའི་མཚན།

༤ གསོལ་བ་འདེབས་སོ་གནས་ལུགས་རང་ཞལ་སྟོན།

༡ ཁྱད་པར་ཟབ་མོ་འོད་གསལ་སྙིང་ཐིག་གི།

༢ ཤིང་རྟ་ཆེན་པོ་མདོ་སྔགས་གླིང་པའི་ཞབས།

༣ བཀའ་དྲིན་མཉམ་མེད་རྩ་བའི་བླ་མ་ལ།

༤ གསོལ་བ་འདེབས་སོ་དོན་གཉིས་ལྷུན་གྲུབ་མཛོད།

༡ སྲིད་ལས་ངེས་པར་འབྱུང་བའི་ཞེན་ལོག་གིས༔

༢ རྡོ་རྗེ་འཕྲེ་མ་དོན་ལྡན་མིག་བཞིན་བསྟེན༔

༣ ཅི་གསུང་བཀའ་བསྒྲུབ་ཟབ་མོའི་ཉམས་ལེན་ལ༔

༤ ཀློམ་རྒྱུང་མེད་པའི་སྒྲུབ་རྩུགས་ཞེ་དྲུས་ཀྱིས༔

༥ ཐུགས་རྒྱུད་དགོངས་པའི་བྱིན་རླབས་འཕོ་བར་ཤོག༔

༦ སྣང་སྲིད་འདས་ཡེ་ནས་འོག་མིན་ཞིང༔

༧ ལྷ་སྔགས་ཆོས་སྐུར་དག་རྫོགས་སྨིན་པའི་འབྲས༔

༨ སྤང་བླང་བྱ་རྩོལ་མེད་པའི་རྫོགས་པ་ཆེ༔

༩ ཤེས་ཉམས་ཡིད་དཔྱོད་ལས་འདས་རིག་པའི་གདངས༔

༡༠ ཆོས་ཉིད་མངོན་་་སུམ་རྗེན་པར་མཐོང་བར་ཤོག༔

༡༡ མཚན་མའི་རྟོག་པ་རྣམ་གྲོལ་འཇའ་ཟེར་སྤྲུབས༔

༡༢ སྐུ་དང་ཐིག་ལེའི་ཉམས་སྣང་གོང་དུ་འཕེལ༔

༡༣ རིག་རྩལ་ལོངས་སྐུའི་ཞིང་ཁམས་ཚད་ལ་ཕེབས༔

༡༤ ཆོས་ཟད་བློ་འདས་ཆེན་པོར་སངས་རྒྱས་ཏེ༔

༡༥ གཞོན་ནུ་བུམ་སྐུར་གཏན་སྲིད་ཟིན་པར་ཤོག༔

༡ ཤིན་ཏུ་རྣལ་འབྱོར་ཉམས་འོག་མ་ཆུད་དེ༔

༢ རགས་ལུས་དྭངས་མའི་དབྱིངས་སུ་མ་གྲོལ་ན༔

༣ ནམ་ཞིག་ཚེ་ཡི་འདུ་བྱེད་བསྡུང་བའི་ཚེ༔

༤ འཆི་བ་འོད་གསལ་ཀ་དག་ཆོས་སྐུར་ཤར༔

༥ བར་དོའི་སྣང་ཆ་ལོངས་སྤྱོད་རྫོགས་སྐུར་གྲོལ༔

༦ ཁྲིགས་ཆོད་ཐོད་རྒལ་ལམ་གྱི་རྩལ་རྫོགས་ནས༔
༧ མཕང་བུ་འཇུག་ལྷ་བུར་གྲོལ་བར་ཤོག༔

༡ གསང་ཆེན་འོད་གསལ་ཐེག་པ་མཆོག་གི་རྩེ༔
༢ སངས་རྒྱས་གཞན་ནས་མི་འཚོལ་ཆོས་སྐུའི་ཞལ༔
༣ མངོན་གྱུར་གདོད་མའི་ས་ལ་མ་གྲོལ་ན༔
༤ མ་སྒོམ་སངས་རྒྱས་ཆོས་ལྷའི་ལམ་མཆོག་ལ༔
༥ བརྟེན་ནས་རང་བཞིན་སྤྲུལ་པའི་ཞིང་ལྷ་དང༔
༦ ཁྱད་པར་པདྨ་འོད་ཀྱི་ཕོ་བྲང་དུ༔
༧ རིག་འཛིན་རྒྱ་མཚོའི་གཙོ་མཆོག་ཨོ་རྒྱན་རྗེས༔
༨ གསང་ཆེན་ཆོས་ཀྱི་དགའ་སྟོན་འགྱེད་པའི་སར༔
༩ སྲས་ཀྱི་ཐུ་བོར་སྐྱེས་ནས་དབུགས་དབྱུང་སྟེ༔
༡༠ མཐའ་ཡས་འགྲོ་བའི་ཉེར་འཚོར་བདག་འགྱུར་ཤོག༔

༡ རིག་འཛིན་རྒྱལ་བ་རྒྱ་མཚོའི་བྱིན་རླབས་དང༔
༢ ཆོས་དབྱིངས་བསམ་མི་ཁྱབ་པའི་བདེན་པ་ཡིས༔
༣ དལ་འབྱོར་རྟེན་ལ་རྫོགས་སྨིན་སྦྱངས་གསུམ་གྱིས༔
༤ རྟེན་འབྲེལ་མངོན་གྱུར་སངས་རྒྱས་ཐོབ་པར་ཤོག༔

ཅེས་ཁ་ཞེ་མེད་པར་གསོལ་བ་སྙིང་ནས་གདབ་བོ༔

དཀྱིལ་དབང་བཞི་བླངས་པ་ནི།

༡ གུ་རུའི་སྨིན་མཚམས་ནས་ཨོཾ་ཡིག་ཆུ་ཤེལ་ལྟ་བུར་འཚེར་བ་ལས་འོད་ཟེར་འཕྲོས༔

༢ རང་གི་སྤྱི་བོ་ནས་ཞུགས༔

༣ ལུས་ཀྱི་ལས་དང་རྩའི་སྒྲིབ་པ་དག༔

༤ སྐུ་རྡོ་རྗེའི་བྱིན་རླབས་ཞུགས༔

༥ བུམ་པའི་དབང་ཐོབ།

༦ བསྐྱེད་རིམ་གྱི་སྣོད་དུ་གྱུར།

༧ རྣམ་སྨིན་རིག་འཛིན་གྱི་ས་བོན་ཐེབས༔

༨ སྤྲུལ་སྐུའི་གོ་འཕང་ཐོབ་པའི་སྐལ་བ་རྒྱུད་ལ་བཞག༔

༡ མགྲིན་པ་ནས་ཨཱཿཡིག་པདྨ་རཱ་ག་ལྟར་འབར་བ་ལས་འོད་ཟེར་འཕྲོས༔

༢ རང་གི་མགྲིན་པ་ནས་ཞུགས།

༣ ངག་གི་ལས་དང་རླུང་གི་སྒྲིབ་པ་དག༔

༤ གསུང་རྡོ་རྗེའི་བྱིན་རླབས་ཞུགས༔

༥ གསང་བའི་དབང་ཐོབ།

༦ བཟླས་བརྗོད་ཀྱི་སྣོད་དུ་གྱུར༔

༧ ཚེ་དབང་རིག་འཛིན་གྱི་ས་བོན་ཐེབས༔

༨ ལོངས་སྤྱོད་རྫོགས་པའི་གོ་འཕང་གི་སྐལ་བ་རྒྱུད་ལ་བཞག༔

༡ ཐུགས་ཀའི་ཧཱུྃ་ཡིག་ནམ་མཁའི་མདོག་ཅན་ལས་འོད་ཟེར་འཕྲོས༔

༢ རང་གི་སྙིང་གནས་ཞུགས།

༣ ཡིད་ཀྱི་ལས་དང་ཐིག་ལེའི་སྒྲིབ་པ་དག༔

༤ ཐུགས་རྡོ་རྗེའི་བྱིན་རླབས་ཞུགས༔

༥ ཤེས་རབ་ཡེ་ཤེས་ཀྱི་དབང་ཐོབ༔

༦ བདེ་སྟོང་ཙཎྜ་ལིའི་སྟོང་དུ་གྱུར༔

༧ ཕྱག་རྒྱའི་རིག་འཛིན་གྱི་ས་བོན་ཐེབས༔

༨ ཆོས་སྐུའི་གོ་འཕང་ཐོབ་པའི་སྐལ་པ་བརྒྱུད་ལ་བཞག༔

༡ སླར་ཡང་ཐུགས་ཀའི་ཧཱུཾ་ལས་ཧཱུཾ་ཡིག་གཉིས་པ་ཞིག་སྐར་མདའ་
འཕངས་པ་བཞིན་དུ་ཆད༔

༢ རང་སེམས་དང་ཐ་དད་མེད་པར་འདྲེས༔

༣ ཀུན་གཞིའི་ལས་དང་ཤེས་བྱའི་སྒྲིབ་པ་སྦྱངས༔

༤ ཡེ་ཤེས་རྡོ་རྗེའི་བྱིན་རླབས་ཞུགས༔

༥ ཚིག་གིས་མཚོན་པ་དོན་དམ་གྱི་དབང་ཐོབ༔

༦ ཀ་དག་རྫོགས་པ་ཆེན་པོའི་སྟོང་དུ་གྱུར༔

༧ ལྷུན་གྲུབ་རིག་འཛིན་གྱི་ས་བོན་ཐེབས༔

༨ མཐར་ཐུག་གི་འབྲས་བུ་ངོ་བོ་ཉིད་སྐུའི་སྐལ་པ་བརྒྱུད་ལ་བཞག༔

དེ་ལྟར་འདོན་བསྒོམ་བྱུང་འཇུག་པས་ལམ་དབང་བླངས་མཐར།

༡ བླ་མའི་ཐུགས་ཀ་ནས་འོད་ཟེར་དམར་པོ་དྲོད་དང་བཅས་པ་ཞིག་ཡལ་གྱིས་

བྱུང་བ་བདག་ཉིད་རྡོ་རྗེ་རྣལ་འབྱོར་མར་གསལ་བའི་སྙིང་ཁར་རིག་པ་ཙམ་
གྱིས་འོད་དམར་གྱི་གོང་བུ་ཞིག་ཏུ་གྱུར་ནས་གུ་རུ་རིན་པོ་ཆེའི་ཐུགས་ཀར
ཐིམ་པས་དབྱེར་མེད་རོ་གཅིག་ཏུ་གྱུར་པར་བསྒོམ།
ཞིང་དམིགས་པ་བསམ་བརྗོད་པ་དང་བྲལ་བའི་ངང་ལ་མཉམ་པར་བཞག་གོ།

དེ་ལས་ལྡང་ནས།

༡ དཔལ་ལྡན་རྩ་བའི་བླ་མ་རིན་པོ་ཆེ།
༢ བདག་གི་སྙིང་གར་པདྨའི་གདན་བཞུགས་ལ།
༣ བཀའ་དྲིན་ཆེན་པོའི་སྒོ་ནས་རྗེས་བཟུང་སྟེ།
༤ སྐུ་གསུང་ཐུགས་ཀྱི་དངོས་གྲུབ་སྩལ་དུ་གསོལ།

༡ དཔལ་ལྡན་བླ་མའི་རྣམ་པར་ཐར་པ་ལ།
༢ སྐད་ཅིག་ཙམ་ཡང་ལོག་ལྟ་མི་སྐྱེ་ཞིང་།
༣ ཅི་མཛད་ལེགས་པར་མཐོང་བའི་མོས་གུས་ཀྱིས།
༤ བླ་མའི་བྱིན་རླབས་སེམས་ལ་འཇུག་པར་ཤོག།
༡ སྐྱེ་བ་ཀུན་ཏུ་ཡང་དག་བླ་མ་དང་།
༢ འབྲལ་མེད་ཆོས་ཀྱི་དཔལ་ལ་ལོངས་སྤྱོད་ནས།
༣ ས་དང་ལམ་གྱི་ཡོན་ཏན་རབ་རྫོགས་ཏེ།
༤ རྡོ་རྗེ་འཆང་གི་གོ་འཕང་མྱུར་ཐོབ་ཤོག།

བཅུ་པ་བསྔོ་བ་ནི།

༡ དགེ་བ་འདི་ཡིས་སྐྱེ་བོ་ཀུན།
༢ བསོད་ནམས་ཡེ་ཤེས་ཚོགས་རྫོགས་ཤིང་།
༣ བསོད་ནམས་ཡེ་ཤེས་ལས་བྱུང་བ།
༤ དམ་པ་སྐུ་གཉིས་ཐོབ་པར་ཤོག།
༡ འགྲོ་ཀུན་དགེ་བ་ཇི་སྙེད་ཡོད་པ་དང་།
༢ བྱས་དང་བྱེད་འགྱུར་དེ་བཞིན་བྱེད་པ་གང་།
༣ བཟང་པོ་ཇི་བཞིན་དེ་འདྲའི་ས་དག་ལ།
༤ ཀུན་ཀྱང་ཀུན་ནས་བཟང་པོར་རེག་གྱུར་ཅིག།

༡ འཇམ་དཔལ་དཔའ་བོས་ཇི་ལྟར་མཁྱེན་པ་དང་།
༢ ཀུན་ཏུ་བཟང་པོ་དེ་ཡང་དེ་བཞིན་ཏེ།
༣ དེ་དག་ཀུན་གྱི་རྗེས་སུ་བདག་སློབ་ཅིང་།
༤ དགེ་བ་འདི་དག་ཐམས་ཅད་རབ་ཏུ་བསྔོ།
༡ དུས་གསུམ་གཤེགས་པའི་རྒྱལ་བ་ཐམས་ཅད་ཀྱིས།
༢ བསྔོ་བ་གང་ལ་མཆོག་ཏུ་བསྔགས་པ་སྟེ།
༣ བདག་གི་དགེ་བའི་རྩ་བ་འདི་ཀུན་ཀྱང་།
༤ བཟང་པོ་སྤྱོད་ཕྱིར་རབ་ཏུ་བསྔོ་བར་བགྱི།

བཅུ་གཅིག་པ་སྨོན་ལམ་ཁྱད་པར་ནི།

1 གང་དུ་སྐྱེས་པའི་སྐྱེ་བ་ཐམས་ཅད་དུ།

2 མཐོ་རིས་ཡོན་ཏན་བདུན་ལྡན་ཐོབ་པར་ཤོག།

3 སྐྱེས་མ་ཐག་ཏུ་ཆོས་དང་འཕྲད་གྱུར་ཅིང་།

4 རྒྱུ་ལ་བཞིན་བསྒྲུབ་པའི་རང་དབང་ཡོད་པར་ཤོག།

5 དེར་ཡང་བླ་མ་དམ་པ་མཉེས་བྱེད་ཅིང་།

6 ཉིན་དང་མཚན་དུ་ཆོས་ལ་སྤྱོད་པར་ཤོག།

7 ཆོས་རྟོགས་ནས་ནི་སྙིང་པོའི་དོན་བསྒྲུབས་ཏེ།

8 ཚེ་དེས་སྲིད་པའི་རྒྱ་མཚོ་བརྒལ་བར་ཤོག།

9 སྲིད་པར་དམ་པའི་ཆོས་རབ་སྟོན་བྱེད་ཅིང་།

10 གཞན་ཕན་བསྒྲུབ་ལ་སྐྱོ་ངལ་མེད་པར་ཤོག།

11 རླབས་ཆེན་གཞན་དོན་ཕྱོགས་རིས་མེད་པ་ཡིས།

12 ཐམས་ཅད་ཆབ་གཅིག་སངས་རྒྱས་ཐོབ་པར་ཤོག། །།

ཅེས་རྫོགས་པ་ཆེན་པོ་ཀློང་ཆེན་སྙིང་ཐིག་གི་སྔོན་འགྲོའི་ངག་འདོན་ཁྲིགས་སུ་བསྡེབས་པ་རྣམ་མཁྱེན་ལམ་བཟང་ འདི་ཉིད་རིག་འཛིན་འཇིགས་མེད་གླིང་པ་སོགས་དམ་པ་དུ་མས་བཀའ་དྲིན་གྱིས་བསྐྱངས་ཤིང་ དམ་ཚིག་ལ་མོས་པ་ཐོབ་པའི་སྔགས་ཀྱི་རྣལ་འབྱོར་པ་ཆེན་པོ་འཇིགས་མེད་འཕྲིན་ལས་འོད་ཟེར་གྱིས་བྲིས་པའི་དགེ་བས། རྗེས་འཇུག་རྣམས་ཀྱིས་བླ་མ་སངས་རྒྱས་སུ་མཐོང་འབྲས་ཀྱིས། རང་རིག་ཀུན་ཏུ་བཟང་པོའི་རང་ཞལ་མངོན་དུ་གྱུར་ནས་འགྲོ་ཁམས་རྒྱ་མཚོ་ལ་ཕན་པ་རྒྱུན་ཆད་མེད་པའི་རྒྱུར་གྱུར་ཅིག། །།